NAVAL GUNS IN FLANDERS
1914–1915

BY

L. F. R.

The Naval & Military Press Ltd

❖

Reproduced by kind permission of the Central Library,
Royal Military Academy, Sandhurst

Published by
The Naval & Military Press Ltd
Unit 10, Ridgewood Industrial Park,
Uckfield, East Sussex,
TN22 5QE England
Tel: +44 (0) 1825 749494
Fax: +44 (0) 1825 765701
www.naval-military-press.com
© The Naval & Military Press Ltd 2004

*In reprinting in facsimile from the original, any imperfections are inevitably reproduced
and the quality may fall short of modern type and cartographic standards.*

HIS MAJESTY'S ARMOURED TRAIN "JELLICOE"

Frontispiece.

CONTENTS

LIST OF ILLUSTRATIONS

PLATES

NAVAL GUNS IN FLANDERS
1914–1915

CHAPTER I

FORTUNE'S FAVOUR

SHORTLY after 8 p.m. on the evening of Thursday, 1914. October 1st, 1914, the two long tables of the Officers' Mess in a naval establishment in a south-eastern county were both full. The assembly represented every branch and calling of His Majesty's Service, combatant and engineer, doctor and pay-master, permanent and temporary, reserve and volunteer. Two of the variety referred to afloat as " Guns," seated together, were engrossed in a heart-to-heart exchange of moans. Each expressed his particular opinion of Dame Fortune and criticized the persistence with which she forgot his existence. They compared their own dull life, sticking it out on the drill-ground and in the class-rooms, endeavouring to train some of those many thousands of recruits, and to prepare them in some fashion for being drafted to sea, upon which

I

1914. domain the envied and fortunate brethren were already playing their part.

Opposite these two sat a younger officer, who was holding forth upon the merits and the endless possibilities of his own new arm of warfare—the Air Service. To a bewildered audience of equally inexperienced messmates around him, he was explaining how he was about to take an ex-cross-Channel packet-boat into the Heligoland Bight, and from her send out aeroplanes to bomb the Germans out of the Kiel Canal, or at any rate destroy their gates.

I hope by now he has learnt the full meaning of the Silent Service.

And so on throughout this assembly of officers almost everyone discussed " shop " in one form or another, for when peace was no more, so likewise went the taboo on that subject.

Of a sudden a resounding crash brought everyone back to a general alertness as the table vibrated under the blow of the " presidential " hammer, and in response to a voice toasting " Gentlemen, the King!" all stood as one and drank. War had brought no change to this old custom, but where previously the repetition of the toast and a prayer, " God bless him!" would have completed the ceremony, now in almost every mind ran the addition " and damn the Hun."

After the assembly was again seated anyone

could rise and leave at will, and with a few remarks 1914.
on the work each had to do during the evening,
both the " Guns " left the mess.

As they passed out through the heavy doors and
across the tiled hall, their Commanding Officer
approached, and addressing one of them, said:
" R——, I want you for a moment " —moving to
the right and so down a passage. When out of
earshot of the hall this officer stopped, and laying
his hand on his junior's arm said: " The C.-in-C.
has just called for an officer for active service. I
have submitted your name. You had better rush
off and pack up some gear, as you will probably
leave in an hour's time."

" Where am I going to ?" asked the junior.

" I do not know exactly, but it is to Belgium,"
was the reply.

" Thank you, sir."

And so did Dame Fortune smile my way at last.

A few minutes ago I had been moaning and
bewailing my fate at having to fag out the boring
existence of a training school; now I was suddenly
pitched into a fever of excitement at the prospect
of immediate active service—" off to the front."

Rushing off, I fled to my room. An hour's grace
and so much to be done ! However, within that
space of time I was again in the hall, with sword
and revolver, wearing my C.O.'s Sam Browne gear,
and kit-bag in hand.

1914. The Commanding Officer was awaiting me, and said " it was approved "; simultaneously another officer approached and said: " Here are your orders."

COPY OF ADMIRALTY TELEGRAM.
[SECRET.]

From Admiralty to Commander-in-Chief, The Nore, dated October 1st, 1914.

" [Priority. Urgent.] Following ratings are to proceed to Antwerp viâ Ostend to-night, sailing in *Engadine* as soon as she can be ready."

(Then followed the details of the draft of seventy active service ratings and the orders to report to the Belgian Government on arrival.)

" To LIEUTENANT (G.)
" For information and guidance.
" RICHARD POORE.
" *Admiral.*"

A thrill of excitement passed through me, and I had bewildered visions of some unexplainable nature.

" The men are assembling now in drill-shed," said my C.O. " I'll see you there later."

Hurriedly I requested the hall porter to forward my mail.

" Where to, sir ?" said he.

"I don't know," I replied, "but Commander 1914. Halahan will tell you later."

"Aye, aye, sir." And with that same old expression of understanding and acknowledgment ringing in my ears, I passed out of the quarters and away to the drill-sheds, where a sense of hustle and subdued excitement filled the air. On one side stood the Commodore, viewing the scene with critical eye. A long queue of bluejackets stretched away through the doors into the square and darkness beyond. At the head of this queue was a collection of officials. Word had quickly and as quietly been passed round that some stunt was on, and that all seamen gunners were to muster at the drill shed in No. 4's, with a clean shift and personal gear in hand. Rumours passed from mouth to mouth, and eagerness to get into the show, whatever it was, soon caused this endless queue of volunteers. Of the many who came forward, a large number had to pass away, for only those who were ready in every detail were selected and marched to one side to be medically examined, then on to be fitted out in field gear, reinspected, and finally passed on to give in name, rating, etc., to the clerk who recorded the full details of each man.

A white cap, no knife, no soap, a faulty bootlace, Off to no collar—even the smallest detail did not escape Front. the quick eye of the police. There was no second

1914. chance, for hundreds waited in the rear ready and equally eager.

Within half an hour seventy ratings had been selected, and were fallen in ready for final inspection.

Meanwhile I had visited the Paymaster and secured seventeen sovereigns,which would probably come in handy before long, and had made arrangements about my affairs.

Two days' iron rations were then served out all round.

" What's the game, Bill ?" " Where are we off to ?" " What's up ?" and similar expressions were to be heard murmured in the excited ranks. At last I was informed that everything was ready, was given the nominal list, and took charge, forming the draft into marching order, and reporting all ready to the Commander.

He in turn reported to the Commodore, who wished us good-luck and Godspeed. I then learnt that we were being despatched to form the crews of six 6-inch guns which had been sent to Antwerp to reinforce the forts.

Rejoining my men, I marched them out of the drill-shed and out into the night. I noticed several forms joining up, and before we had proceeded many yards on the way to the dockyard gate the party had increased considerably in numbers.

Halting before the gate, I called the roll and 1914. passed each of my own men through; the extras disappeared into the darkness, their last effort foiled. Once again we moved off, and the gates behind us closed with a bang. It seemed as if this sudden clanging of the gates resounding in the still night air had startled the senses of most of us into realizing that we were alone and on some venture into the unknown, certainly for the men, who as yet were not aware of their errand. The moment seemed to require relief, so I called for a song, and at once the dockyard walls resounded with the refrain of " Tipperary." We did not have far to go, and shortly before 11 p.m. boarded the launch, which bore us downstream on the way to our transport. Collecting the men together, I informed them of our destination and our errand—a surprising piece of news, at first received with much excitement, but soon followed by silence, for each had his own thoughts to occupy him, either of his own future or of those who were left behind.

An hour's silent journey brought us alongside the *Engadine*, which till lately had been a cross-Channel packet-boat. She was completing with coal and busily preparing for her journey. I got the men comfortably settled for the night, and then tried to sleep myself, but with little success, for excitement was too intense.

1914 By 1 a.m. the *Engadine* slipped from her buoy
and out of the black harbour. On our way we
were to pick up Lieutenant Ridler of the *Severn*,
who was to join the party, and had been so informed by wireless. A mist lay over the sea, but
we eventually found and picked him up at the
Girdler; unfortunately, however, the ship herself
was allowed to drift on to a sand-bank and delayed us.

At daylight the mist was quite thick, but we
continued on our journey as fast as the turbines
could drive us. Hot coffee and biscuits was served
out and the draft detailed into seven sections. As
we were approaching Ostend the following signal
was received by wireless, adding greatly to our
excitement and making everyone even more determined to do his best.

Admiralty to " Engadine."

First
Lord's
Message. " First Lord wishes representatives of the Royal
Navy now going into action at Antwerp good-
fortune and Godspeed. The cause which they are
to serve is the preservation of the National Life
of the Belgian people, who are in the extreme
distress of a cruel, terrible, and unprovoked attack.
A million men in the British Isles now getting
ready to take part in the struggle will watch the
feat of arms expected from the small number of
naval ratings employed."

To this we made reply :

" Engadine " to Admiralty.

" To First Lord.

  " Officers and men now in *Engadine, en route* for Antwerp, wish to send their heartiest thanks for, and to express their cordial appreciation of, your message conveying such encouraging attention."

Later in the forenoon we made out the marks of Ostend, and proceeded up the harbour about 11 a.m., berthing alongside the Railway Quay. A Oct. 2nd. train was waiting for us, so we disembarked at once, exchanging cheers with the crew of the transport and also with the populace, a great crowd of which were gathered round the precincts of the station.

  " Third return Chatham, please, miss !" shouted the wag.

  " Berlin and b—— the Kaiser !" replied the rest.

  And so on, with compartments labelled " Berlin " and hoglike caricatures of the war lord, we steamed out midst cheers, and so forward to the unknown. Our first stop was at Bruges at 12.30 p.m. Immediately the train had pulled up a crowd of civilians and guards, men and women, rushed along to greet us, bringing food, fruits, and drink. This

1914. wholesale display of kindness and hospitality was at first most embarrassing, but not so much so as the one great question which was on everyone's lips: " Thank God, the English have come ! But how many are coming, and where are all the others ?" Their anxiety was terribly apparent, and yet there was only one thing to say: " Many thousands more are following behind us." We could but give some encouragement, though in reality we knew not whether thousands or none were to follow; in fact, we knew less of what was behind than what was in front of us, and that was very little.

One thing, however, was quite apparent —that if this sort of drinking and feasting continued all the way to Antwerp the men would soon be all intoxicated, so a stop had to be put to the former part of the menu. That afternoon we continued a very slow journey eastwards along the Dutch frontier loop via Lokeren, and so on to St. Nicholas, stopping at most stations, where we always met with the same everlasting questions and with the same gifts.

At St. Nicholas we had a prolonged wait; everywhere things were busy, and many trains were going westward. A troop train full of Belgian soldiers passed us, and as soon as they saw who we were, they gave a terrific cheer and yell of " Les Anglais !"

Off again, we slowly moved east, passing crowds 1914
of soldiers and a great quantity of military material,
earthworks and barbed-wire entanglements, and so
on, till about 6 p.m. we passed the forts and
stopped at the station of St. Anne. Here we were
told to disembark and to board a ferry at the
quay. I noticed a large pile of boxes and luggage
under a guard on the quay, and was informed that
it was the baggage of the Queen, who was to leave
that night.

It was by now quite dark, but the city was Antwerp.
brilliantly lit, though, in spite of this, the reflec-
tions of the flashes away to the south showed the
sources of the constant rumble, as the guns continued their work.

And so, at last, was heard the sound of battle at
hand and we were thrilled with excitement. We
crossed the Scheldt and disembarked, but had to
wait for a Belgian Staff Officer to join us, who was
to show the way to our quarters. When in half
an hour's time he arrived, we set out on our march
through the city, till in its eastern quarter we
came to the so-called barracks wherein our men
were to be lodged for the night. Then things
began to happen. No one ever knows how a
crowd will spring up in a city street, apparently
by magic, and here suddenly we were being surrounded by a crowd of women, men, and children.

" Vivent les Anglais !" they shouted. " Vive

ANTWERP

SCALE
0   ¼   ½   ¾   1 Mile
0   1 Kilometre
Railway   Roads

l'Angleterre ! A-ah, ça va bien ! Ils arrivent." 1914.
The men called in answer: " Cheer-o, monsoo !
Vive Belgique !"

Before very long we were a surging mass instead
of only seventy sailors, the crowd disguising our
small number. Again, and even more eagerly, the
same questions were asked: " How many are
coming, and where are they ?"

But to our small band the welcome was so
whole-hearted from these people who had met us
at their gates, that we all felt very proud of being
Britishers. It was good to feel that Britain had
not failed her friends, though the obligation were
only a moral one. Yes, one felt proud as never
before.

Our quarters consisted of two bare rooms on the
first floor of an equally bare large building. We
were able to arrange for hot coffee and some
biscuits, and then, tired by the day's journey,
most stretched out on the floor and tried to get
some sleep. Ridler and myself then rejoined the
Staff Officer in his car and went off to the Headquarters. Here things seemed to be somewhat
busy, and we could not get any immediate instructions, so decided to go out and get some dinner
first, for it was now 9 p.m.

The Hôtel St. Antoine was recommended, so
thither we went, and were very thankful for a
decent warm dinner after such a tiring journey.

CHAPTER II

THE EVACUATION OF ANTWERP

1914. My instructions were to get in touch with a certain naval officer who was already in Antwerp with other naval guns and men; so it seemed advisable to see what our Embassy could do, as they were quartered at the time in the Hôtel St. Antoine. We eventually got in touch with one of the Secretaries, and after a further short wait were requested to go in, as His Excellency wished to speak to us. On entering, we were very cordially greeted by an elderly gentleman, who then said:

" Well, gentlemen, I am sorry to tell you that you have come too late. The authorities have just decided that the city is to be evacuated. The Belgian Field Army is leaving now for the west with His Majesty the King, and only the garrison are remaining to guard the city and cover the retreat."

He told us that the majority of the forts in the southern sector of the outer ring of forts had already been blown to bits by heavy guns and had fallen, and that it was certain that the city could not be saved from capture.

This was very sad news for us indeed; there 1914.
seemed to be no time to waste thinking about it,
but to attempt to find the senior British naval
officer present in the city and report.

After parting with His Excellency we returned
to the hotel lounge, and then I caught sight of a
British naval officer. An exchange of greetings
and names showed that this was the very person
whom we sought. He had crossed from England
during the preceding month with six 4·7-inch guns
for the same purpose as ourselves, but they proved
much too feeble; however, he obtained the necessary permission and had mounted them on railway
bogies, forming a couple of armoured trains. The
idea was first tried with one gun which was mounted
on the bogie of a large wagon, and upon com-
pletion about the middle of September proved
quite a success. All six guns were subsequently
so mounted, and by this time were out in action
daily, forming two complete trains of three guns,
two engines, and two magazines each, all protected
by steel plating ⅜ inch thick, sufficient to stop
splinters and rifle bullets. We learnt that our six
6-inch guns were in a certain engineering yard,
but that their use in the matter of reinforcing the
forts was considered negligible.

He had heard rumours of the anticipated evacu-
ation, but ours was the first definite news which
reached him, and he had as yet received no orders

1914. on the subject. At this moment Rear-Admiral Oliver appeared upon the scene and inquired at what hour the armoured trains would be ready to leave Antwerp for the west, for we were all to clear out as soon as possible; it was thereupon decided that all could and would be ready at 4 a.m. next morning. It was now midnight, so I borrowed a car and went to the men's quarters to warn them to be ready. The whole city seemed to be full of cars, and every officer owned one. One hardly saw an officer on foot at all. Our men were all dead to the world, tired out. But I told them to be ready to fall in at 3 a.m. Returning to the hotel, I asked for a room, and was soon asleep on top of the bed. After a couple of hours' rest the night porter called us and brought a welcome cup of coffee. Arriving at the barracks, I found the men ready, so we fell-in at once and started our march across the city.

Once more in pitch darkness, but guided by our car, three-quarters of an hour's marching brought us to the Gare des Dames, where we found the armoured trains. The engines were still shunting about, filling with coal and water, and a certain amount of confusion prevailed. I divided the men into six parties putting one in each gun wagon.

By 4.30 the trains were ready, and we were about to start on our return journey to Ostend, when the order came to " stop." From somewhere 1914. a message had arrived, and the Rear-Admiral said the trains and men were to remain where they were in readiness for the time being.

Ridler went off to try and collect the 6-inch guns, and to see what was possible with them, whilst I accompanied the Rear-Admiral back to the hotel, where we got the news from the Embassy that the First Lord of the Admiralty and Staff had left London for Antwerp, and were expected about midday; meanwhile we were to wait.

In the interval it was decided to get on with the work with the 6-inch guns. They were to be placed in positions chosen between the forts of the inner ring as part of the defences being built there, mounted on crossed double 10-inch girders sunk in the soil. The Antwerp Emergency Company started the work at once, and Ridler took over the task of superintending.

The First Lord arrived at the hotel about 1 p.m. Churchill Seeing me, he asked whether I belonged to the at Antwerp. Royal Naval Division, and, learning the nature of my errand, wanted to know how long it would take. He appeared satisfied with the estimate I gave, and remarked that " we were going to hold out."

This was the first news I had heard that the newly formed Naval Brigades were to arrive in this neighbourhood.

2

1914.   However, with the Staff came more details, and also rumours of the despatch of troops of the British Army.

Our own particular job was clear: we could continue the work begun on the 6-inch guns and the 4·7 trains could carry on with their normal programme. These latter had done nothing during this day but remain in readiness to leave, a diversion from their usual activities which caused their local Headquarters to ask " Why ?" That was smoothed over when all was explained and orders for the following day's work were issued to them.

Commandant Lefevre, a Belgian Engineer Officer who had been largely instrumental in the building of the trains, joined us at dinner in the evening, as also Captain Servais, a retired Belgian Artilleryman who commanded one of the sections of the armoured trains. That night we slept at the Oct. 4th. latter's house. Next morning Ridler took some of the men and continued with the 6-inch, whilst I split the remainder up amongst the 4·7 guns. Till now Lieutenant-Commander Littlejohns was actually in charge of both trains, and generally went out in one section, whilst Captain Servais took charge of the other. From the beginning the guns had been manned by British naval gunlayers assisted by volunteer Belgians. It was now decided that my bluejackets should assist, whilst I went out with Littlejohns to help him, and eventually take over the train to give him more freedom to go to Head- 1914. quarters, and so on.

Leaving at 5 a.m., we took his section out viâ Wilryck and prepared for firing at Waerloos.

The methods of laying and training the guns were most primitive, for up till lately all firings out to the southward of the Nethe had been direct. Now that the Germans had advanced and were actually assaulting the city's defences, cover was necessary, and in such flat country firing had to be indirect, or blind.

A position was chosen where the map showed a straight piece of line, the line of the rails being taken as the zero for training. Bearing and ranges were taken off the map. The guns were laid to the elevation corresponding to the range required, and a bearing arc was painted round the pedestal, the zero pointer being a plumb-line slung from beneath the mounting.

With such means success in indirect laying was a matter of luck, and it was obvious that calibration and greatly improved ideas were necessary.

As soon as the train stopped, telephone communication was always established with the Headquarters under which the train was working at the time, and so kept in touch ready to fire whenever required.

The target was a battery position to the southeast of Duffel at a range of 5,000 yards, and over

1914. this area a steady fire was placed. A hostile captive balloon was observed to ascend, so I asked Littlejohns if I could try and down it. We opened fire on it with long-range shrapnel, and after four rounds it was hurriedly hauled down. However, it had time to see us, so we retreated a few hundred yards; and sure enough, after a lapse of some minutes, our previous position was subjected to a searching but weak fire from some battery.

About midday we advanced beyond Waerloos, stopped just short of the bridge over the line, and opened fire on another battery at 6,500 yards. The First Lord and his Staff arrived during this performance. He remarked: " We cannot have too many of these trains." Two members of the Staff inquired whether the firing-line was visible; we informed them that if they went on top of the bridge in front of us they would be able to get a good view. They went out, and hardly reached their destination when shell began falling in the neighbourhood of the train and shrapnel crackled overhead. I do not suppose those officers had run so fast for many a day, for their time for the distance separating them from the shelter of the train was remarkably fast.

As for myself, it was the first time I had been under fire. I heard an awful shriek overhead, so dived into a ditch alongside. It did not take very long to learn that a shrieking shell had already

passed overhead and out of danger. A shell which 1914.
will be unfortunately near one gives little or no
time to get clear after one catches the first sound
of its shrieking passage through the air.

A Taube appeared high up and coming towards
us, the first hostile aircraft I had seen. Determined to have a shot at a Hun myself, I laid the
6-pounder anti-aircraft gun with which we were
fitted, and opened fire on him.

Perhaps he did not expect that sort of reception,
for he immediately banked steeply to the right
and went off home; however, he no doubt saw us
and would report our position, so we again withdrew the train a few hundred yards.

Most of the houses around us had already been
deserted, but some of the inhabitants still lingered.

That evening Littlejohns and myself met Temporary Colonel Sir P. Girouard at the Antoine and
dined with him. The sad state of the white shirt
and collar I had worn when leaving England was
too apparent, so he offered me a khaki substitute
in lieu from his kit.

Early next morning the train went out again, Oct. 5th.
and this time I took charge of one section in place
of Littlejohns, who remained in Antwerp for a
conference on the question of the 6-inch guns. It
was decided to abandon the idea of placing the
guns in the positions chosen, but to place the
girders on a railway bogie and mount the guns

similarly to the 4·7's. This was rather an experiment, for we could not estimate whether the
recoil would be so severe as to prevent the gun
being fired much out of the fore and aft line of the
truck, for fear of upsetting it.

I took my section out viâ Vieu Dieu and
stopped at Kleine Meil, on the Brussels line, in a
position which was screened by a dense wood over
which we could fire. Headquarters telephoned the
position of two targets which were to be engaged—
thé bridge over the River Nethe east of Lierre,
which village had been evacuated by the Belgians
and was being occupied by the advancing German
troops; and the Ander-Stad-Farm on the southern
bank of the Nethe, more to the westward. I was
informed that the Belgians had all crossed this
river and were taking up positions along its western
bank as far west as Willebroeck. The above farm
was a little shelter from which the Germans would
launch an attack to cross the river.

I opened fire on these two objectives and continued a slow bombardment at irregular intervals.
In the early part of the forenoon a battery commenced searching for us, but, beyond an occasional
uncomfortably close one, most of the shell did not
fall close enough to look dangerous, so I held on
to our screened position.

In the late afternoon an order came to return
and go out on the Lierre line, and from there open

fire on the Duffel Bridge over the Nethe and on the 1914.
" S " bend of the river immediately west of Lierre,
as Germans were massing to attack at these two
places. Arriving at a point on the line marked
K. 7 on the map, which denotes the position of the
seventh kilometre sign-post, I opened fire and
continued till dusk, when we returned to Antwerp
for the night. Thus my first days of independent
work came to a close.

It was the general principle that the train should
not work at night, when the flashes would draw
hostile fire on their surroundings and so interfere
with the passage of reliefs and food, etc., moving
up to the front, and also stray shells were liable
to cut the rails in rear and cause a derailment in
the dark.

During this afternoon a French armoured train
joined us, and opened fire on Walheim. It was a
very good unit, mounting two short 7·5-inch guns
of considerable ranging power, but before firing
the mountings had to be secured to the rails and
supports rigged out from the truck so as to hold
it all in place; so that it was not mobile as we were,
for we could fire when in motion at any point of the
compass.

The methods and customs of our Ally amused
the men, but this amusement caused that light-
hearted gaiety which is quite irresistible in the
endeavour to surmount trifling difficulties in a

THE LIERRE DISTRICT

SCALE

X Indicate Gun Positions   O Indicate Targets

foreign land. In like circumstances the British 1914.
bluejacket is at his best, and volumes could be
filled with the anecdotes of their adventures in
Belgian and French villages. " Knowalls " who
for ever are trying to introduce the universal
language could certainly draw some useful hints
from the " blue " in a strange land. He is soon
equally at home in China, Pacific Islands, Amazon,
or in the wilds of Africa.

The only thing which seemed to stump their
ideas was the alarming manner in which the children
so soon picked up the language. Grown-ups, yes;
they of course would learn it in time; but the
fluency and speed of the children's jabber was
beyond them.

Somehow they got on much quicker with the
womenfolk—a subject for the student; but the
whole-hearted welcome admiration and wonder-
ment of the womenfolk for the men, and their own
patient sufferings and hardships, seemed to produce
a sort of favourable medium.

At daylight next day I took the section out Oct. 6th.
again and stopped at Kleine Meil. Our first target
was again the bridge east of Lierre, upon which
we opened fire. I learnt that during the preceding
night the enemy had built pontoon bridges across
the river and had attacked just west of Lierre,
succeeding in forcing the Belgians out of their
trenches. This advance was checked and the

1914. trenches cleared by the arrival of the **Royal Naval Brigade** under General Paris, belonging to the Royal Naval Division. These fine soldiers from the sea had attacked as soon as they arrived on the field, and though they retook the lost positions, had not been able to force the Germans off the north-western bank of the river.

Our line now ran along the main road between Lierre and Duffel Bridge.

Early in the forenoon I got orders to return to Waesdoirck and go out on the Lierre line. At the first place I picked up Girouard and Littlejohns and whilst passing through Bouchout Station one of the gun bogies was derailed, causing a delay. All round this area were many London buses drawn up by the roadside. They had come straight from the London streets and had been used to rush up the Naval Division from Dunkerque. We were reminded of home by the brilliant advertisements of the theatres, etc., such as the one I photographed with Girouard at the controls and Littlejohns as the conductor.

We left the derailed bogie behind with a salvage party and went on with the other two guns to a position behind the Donk Wood beyond K. 8. In this position we were in front of most of the field artillery, which were barking away on both quarters and only a mile from our own Marines holding the line in front of us west of Lierre.

GARE ST. NICHOLAS.

THE GEARLESS BUS AT BOUCHOUT.

To face page 26.

Our first target was a double battery of field- 1914. guns which a Belgian balloon observed to be in action in a position at Blijenhoek, 2,000 yards to the south-west of Lierre.   We opened fire with lyddite and shrapnel, and after half an hour we were informed that the enemy had ceased fire and were moving away.   We were told to open fire on the pontoon bridges used in last night's attack, so a slow bombardment was directed on this area. After about twenty minutes we must have been spotted by the balloons, for a battery opened on us with shell of a medium calibre.   Their first salvo straddled us—one shell landed and exploded 100 yards on one side, and another as much on the other, whilst one landed—a " dud "—in the ditch alongside the train.   We did not wait for more, but went back to K. 7, and from there watched the continued shelling of our previous position, which made several breaks in the rails.   At this time further orders arrived to fire at once on Lierre Station and the north-western portion of the village itself, as the Germans were debouching from this part and massing in the station area ready for an attack.   Lyddite was fired on these areas slowly for the remainder of the forenoon, during which time the derailed bogie arrived and joined in.

At noon we had to return to Antwerp for water, and on the way passed Ridler, who had succeeded

1914. in getting the first 6-inch mounted, and was on
his way to test it with a few trial shots at the Hun.
A second 6-inch was completing and expected out
to join him. This was a good piece of work, for
only forty-eight hours' continuous working sufficed
to mount the two.

Passing through the inner line of forts, we met
the other Brigades of the Naval Division, who
were busy digging themselves in, on the trench
system between the forts. In front of this system
was about 75 yards of solid barbed-wired entanglements, and a further 50 yards' width of " too-de-
loos " in front—a nest of pointed wooden pegs,
points up.

All the area in front for hundreds of yards was
being systematically cleared of woods, houses, and
villages to leave a clear open space over which
the enemy would have to advance if he got so
far in.

Whilst the engines were preparing to go out
again Littlejohns and I visited the General Headquarters, and there I met the Commander-in-Chief,
General De Guise. He congratulated us upon the
apparent success of the shoot that morning against
the double battery.

We were soon out again on the Lierre line, and
from K. 7 I opened fire on that part of the northern
bank west of Lierre where the pontoons landed.
This continued for a short while until a further

order to concentrate on the Duffel Bridge arrived. 1914.
It was said that the attack on Lierre had been
checked, but that another was being pressed on
our right flank at Duffel.

All the afternoon we kept up a steady fire upon
this area until dusk arrived, when we had to
return and try to obtain a replenishment of the
greatly depleted shell supply, for the heavy day's
firing had caused a big expenditure. Whilst
searching round trying to find where the reserve
trucks had been shunted to, I got a message that
I was to report at once at the Antoine.

There I met Girouard, who said that the Germans
had succeeded in forcing back the Belgians on our
right, and that we were to clear out with what
guns we could save, and destroy the remainder.
We were to leave at 11 p.m., so there was plenty
to do to get the trains all connected up ready to
depart.

There was only one way out, which we hoped
might be still clear—*i.e.*, over the Boom Bridge—
but the Germans had been in sight of it for two
days, and by now might be holding the southern
bank. However, it was our only chance, and
once across the bridge only derailment could stop
us. It was not till 11.30 that we eventually got
away with both the 4·7 trains, for the 6-inch were
held up still at Hoboken, but were to follow.

All went well till we reached Wilryck Station.

1914. The night had become as red as day, as the glare of the burning houses and buildings everywhere mounted to the sky in huge streaks of light, showing where everything was being blown up, burnt, and destroyed in the endeavour to open up the area in front of the inner defences. The roads were packed with a seething mass of men, women, and children of all ages, household effects, and hundreds of soldiers, all streaming towards the city in head-long retreat before the threatened advance of the Huns.

It was such a picture as only an artist could give us on a canvas. No man is more tender to the helpless than the British " blue," no one more cheerful; and not one of us but felt his heart wrung by the infinite pathos of this terror-stricken mob.

As we drew up at Wilryck the station-master started waving his arms in frantic gesticulations, and told us that we could not go on viâ Contich, as that village was already occupied by the enemy. There was still one way left by which we could reach the Boom Bridge—the single line round by the bank of the Scheldt viâ Hoboken.

It was now just past midnight, and our chances
Oct. 7th. of getting away in the darkness seemed to be getting thinner and thinner. However, we started off on our new line, but had hardly got a mile before we were brought up all standing with a grinding of brakes. Jumping out to see what was

in the way, we found about a hundred trucks and 1914. wagons barring our path, all in the various stages of unloading but quite deserted by the owners, the Naval Divisions, and not another engine in sight. Such a load was beyond the power of our own two engines, and even then we could not push all this lot out in front of us, so after a few moments' consideration we decided to abandon the train and walk to Hoboken, where if we could not get out by rail, we could cross the river and get away to the west on foot.

The railway-side was strewn with all manner of articles and food-stuffs. Littlejohns borrowed a bicycle, and as soon as we met a road made off for the city. Girouard took charge and led the way along the line, all stumbling over the rails and sleepers in the darkness, but trying to keep as quiet as possible, with a very much open eye to the left for the enemy, who might pop up at any moment on our flank. Behind us the villages were burning, whilst to the south the roar and flashes of the guns showed where the battle was raging.

Half an hour's tramp in this fashion brought us to the Hoboken yards where the 6-inch were still held up. After a certain amount of signalling and arguing, we persuaded a tug to come alongside and take us all across to the western bank.

When once landed, everyone, I fancy, gave vent

1914. to a sigh of relief.   There we found a small esta-
minet and were able to stir the inmates into
activity, getting them to serve out a tot of schnapps
to each man, Girouard signing a chit on behalf of
the British Government for the cost.   The inn-
keeper seemed quite content, saying, " Oh, the
English will pay."   It was bitterly cold, but the
liquor put fresh life into us all.   Once again we
set out, and eventually brought up in a village
named Cruybeke.   The place was full of Belgian
soldiers, from whom we learnt the whereabouts of
their local Headquarters.

There we learnt the latest news from Antwerp,
and as there did not seem to be any urgent need
to hurry on, we sought out a friendly barn, and
all lay down for an hour's rest.   From the smell
of the place it must have been sacks of fertilizer
upon which we lay.

At 4 a.m. we again visited the Headquarters and
got into telephone touch with the city.   They
said that Contich was clear of Germans, and that
the Boom Bridge was still in our hands, so there
still seemed a chance of retrieving our trains if
we retraced our steps and tried once more.   This
course was decided on, so I shook up the men and
returned to Hoboken.   There we got the 6-inch
under way, whilst Girouard left us and went into
the city to find Littlejohns, who was to follow in
the 4·7 trains.

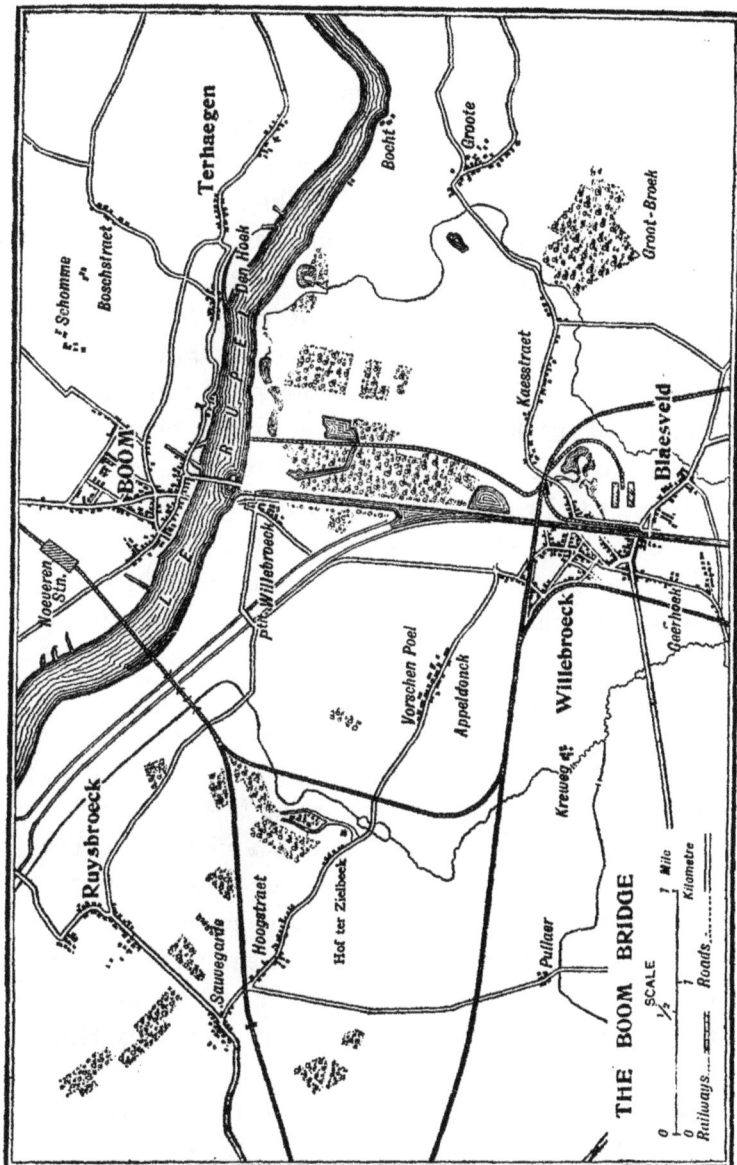

THE BOOM BRIDGE

Terhaegen

Schomme

Boschstraet

Bocht

Groote

Groot-Broek

Stal Hoek

Kaesstraet

BOOM

Blaesveld

Noeveren Stn.

Pte Willebroeck

Vorschen Poel

Willebroeck

Appeldonck

Geerhoek

Ruysbroeck

Kreweg

Sauwegarde

Hoogstraet

Hof ter Zielbeek

Pullaer

SCALE
0   ½   1 Mile
0   Kilometre
Railways.....
Roads.........

1914.   By the time all was ready it was almost midday, and once again we got to Wilryck Station,
which was now deserted. Farther on Contich
hove in sight, but not a rail had been touched,
and we began to doubt whether the Huns had
ever been there at all. What was more likely
was that the personnel had deserted the station,
and when Wilryck could get no reply had assumed
the worst. We steamed slowly on, keeping a
good lookout for a broken rail, and a better one
for a surprise from the enemy from the east, till
at last the bridge itself came in sight.

Continuing slowly, we saw Belgians working
there, so that seemed hopeful; but the man in the
signal-box had had no orders about us, and would
not give us the signal, so we jumped out, put it
to " clear " and passed on.

The   As soon as we arrived at the bridge we could see
Escape. it clear and intact, so the throttles were opened
wide, and we were soon racing as fast as possible,
over the river, across the canal, and on into the
trees, all eyes on the watch for a sign of the
Huns or a broken line, but not a sign did we
see. At last we turned round to the west and on
to Puers, when everyone let out a yell of delight,
for we reckoned we were clear at last, this time
with our own guns.

As we passed over the canal at Tamese we saw
the Belgians entrenching on its northern banks,

6-INCH GUNS AT OSTEND.

To face page 34.

waiting for an attack from the south; our appear- 1914.
ance from that direction was a surprise. Once
we passed again through the awful spectacle of the
retreating masses, all moving west, till at last we
stopped in the station of St. Nicholas. Here we
were to wait and see if Girouard and Littlejohns
got through with the 4·7's. After some trying hours
they arrived, and at last we were complete. They
had been through even more exciting experiences,
for after the other guns left behind had been
destroyed, they got to the Boom Bridge only just
in time to get over and away before it was destroyed
by the retreating Belgian Engineers.

During the night we joined up together and left Ostend
for Ostend, arriving there the following evening, again.
after a very slow and jerky journey.

We learnt that Antwerp had capitulated during
that day, for the bombardment of the city which
had begun the night we left had continued,
and the destruction of the city seemed certain.
The Germans were attacking the inner defences,
and the forts there were being demolished one by
one. The Belgian Field Army and Naval Division
got across the river, though part of the latter
stayed till the Germans were actually fighting on
the wire entanglements, and then the garrison
alone remained behind to cover the retreat and
destroy all they could. Awful tales of these last
few hours were told in Ostend on their arrival   As

1914. soon as possible we got some food for the men, for we had all been without supplies for two days, and then got a meal ourselves at the Hôtel des Thermes. Ostend itself was in an awful state of chaos: the Belgian Field Artillery were moving through and to the west; the remnants of the Naval Division were arriving at intervals and embarking for England; the 4th Army Corps under General Rawlinson was disembarking and moving to the south-east to cover the retreat; whilst hundreds of thousands of refugees were seeking shelter and any possible means of putting the biggest distance between themselves and the Huns, fleeing into France or embarking in any old " ditcher " whose exorbitant price they could pay for a trip to England.

On Saturday, October 10th, orders were received from England to send the guns to Dover, so I had to prepare them for dismounting and ready to be hoisted out into a transport. By 2 p.m. all were ready, and then orders came to belay, so I had to replace them and get ready for service again.

CHAPTER III

THE FIRST BATTLE OF YPRES

I.—YPRES.

I⊤ transpired that the 4th Army wanted all the guns it could get, and here were some ready, so a telegram or two soon arranged matters. Towards evening General Rawlinson sent for Littlejohns, and told him to send a train to co-operate with the 7th Division—General Capper.

Littlejohns sent for me and explained the affair, and offering me the job, said I could take a 4·7 section. During the evening I arranged the train, selected my own full three crews of bluejackets, and two engines with their own mechanics. We also filled up with what few tinned provisions I could find and plenty of ammunition. By 3 a.m. all was ready; I had my charts, and had orders to report to the Headquarters, which would be found at a place called Eeringhem. *Ordre de marche* and red-tape held me up, so that it was 4.30 before I could get clear of Ostend Station, but once again we were off to action somewhere— this time with all hearts full of pride, for we were to be with the grand old B.E.F.

37

1914.   An hour's journeying brought us to the destination, which we found deserted except for a few civilians, who said the English had moved on. We followed, but they were not at Istexghem, so I telephoned to Thourout and found that British Cavalry were there. Meanwhile I was able to persuade the kind lady at the hotel to give us all a cup of hot coffee. We moved on to Thourout, and from there got into touch with the Headquarters of the 3rd Cavalry—Brigadier-General Byng being at Coolscamp.

Whilst I was explaining the situation a despatch-rider arrived with an order. It appeared that there had been some mistake made in the original orders I got before leaving Ostend.

This order read:

To Officer Commanding Armoured Train.

" Please despatch the armoured train immediately to Ghent. On arrival there report to Major-General Capper, commanding the 7th Division.
" (Signed)   M. F. G——,
   " *Lieut.-Colonel, 3rd Cavalry Division.*"

At the same time General Byng himself arrived and explained the mistake in the original orders, so I at once set off to Bruges and on to Bellem, where I picked up an officer of the Grenadiers. Arriving at St. Pierre Station, Ghent, about

4.30 p.m., I found the Divisional Headquarters 1914 installed in the Hôtel de Ville, and arrived in time to join in the afternoon tea. Everyone was busy working on maps and writing out orders, but in the end I met the General and reported, explaining what sort of engine of warfare I commanded. He gave me the details and explained the withdrawal of his Division that evening from the precincts of Ghent towards Bruges, and told me to go to Melle and report there to Brigadier-General Lawford, commanding the 22nd Brigade, who would give me orders as to how to co-operate with him. Lying on his table was a German helmet, which I was in the act of admiring when General Capper remarked:

" That is the Division's first trophy. Would you like it ?"

Flabbergasted, I replied: " Yes."

" Then it is yours," said he; " take it, with the good wishes of the 7th Division."

That helmet is now one of my proudest possessions.

Accompanied by a Staff Officer, we left Ghent after dark and went as far as a point from In Action whence we had to strike across country on foot to at Ghent. find the Brigade Headquarters, falling into ditches and climbing fences, eventually bringing up at a most insignificant cottage, where we found the General. He explained his plan of withdrawal

GENERAL CONDITIONS
Oct. 10th-11th.

German Cavalry..........
German Corps...........
Railways................

and his wishes that from 8.15 p.m. I should open 1914.
fire for an hour, one gun searching each of the
three roads from Oordegen, Oosterzel, and Muelte,
whilst at 8.30 he was to commence retiring from
his position.

We returned to the train and carried out the
programme, afterwards returning to Ghent.   There
I found the French evacuating their hospital, and
they asked me to carry away a load of the effects
of their wounded, which I loaded into a truck and
eventually left with the railway authorities at
Bruges.   I bought a quantity of loaves for the men,
and at 11.30 p.m. proceeded to Aeltre for the night.

I was to report to Divisional Headquarters at
Hansbeke next morning, but on arriving there at
6 a.m. found that they had left, and were then
on their way to Bellem, so I returned there to
wait for them.   At 10 a.m. they arrived, and on Oct. 12th.
reporting, the General said: " Well done ! You
may probably have held up an attack at the
moment of our retirement." He directed me Scouting.
to advance to the canal bridge at Landegem to
communicate with the outposts and patrols there,
and co-operate with them as I thought fit.
Arriving there, I got into touch with them,
and at 1.15 p.m. advanced out with one gun
to Helsendrieck to look for a sign of any enemy
patrols. Nothing turned up by 2 p.m., so I
returned with that report. An hour later I

1914. advanced again as far as Tronchiennes, and here they said that the Germans were passing round to the north of Ghent in large numbers, and that a Uhlan patrol had been sighted north-east of this village itself. I saw the Belgian Engineers blow up the Assel Bridge over the canal in front of me, so returned and reported again at Hansbeke.

The train now required water, so we returned to Bruges, where I ran into an awful chaos of traffic, and that small evolution took six hours before I got clear again. Shortly before midnight we got into position just west of the Landegem Canal Bridge to support our cavalry, who were detailed together with the Belgian Guides, to hold it that night. It was a pitch-black night and very quiet, and one could almost imagine phantom Huns watching from the other side of the canal as I walked along the bank in my search for the Cavalry Headquarters. As it was, I almost fell into a trench which was dug into the railway embankment, wherein were installed a section of the Northumberland Yeomanry. I eventually found the farm which was their Headquarters, but learnt that they had all moved off some time before, the section on the railway not having retired with the main body.

Returning to the bridge, I found the Belgian Guides and spent some time with them, but as they were about to retire, I told the Yeomanry to

THE CREW OF THE TRAIN.

To face page 42.

get aboard, and we retired also. We passed 1914.
Bellem, picking up a horsebox with a fine charger
in it and a wagon full of regimental impedi-
menta, then retired to Aeltre, and reported by Oct. 13th.
telephone to the Divisional Headquarters, which
were now at Thielt. Things must have been very
busy there, for it was not till the noon that orders
arrived to send the troops across country to
Roulers, and to proceed myself to Bruges and
there await orders.

During the forenoon a Taube flew over us very
low, so we opened fire with the 6-pounder and all
our rifles; he seemed to get very annoyed, dived
and dodged about, and flew away to the south-
east, still very low. At Bruges orders came to
report to the Corps Headquarters at Roulers. I
learnt that all our forces had reached Roulers, and
that the Germans had entered Thielt, though our
Cavalry were still working about Thourout; Uhlan
patrols were reported as having been seen all over
the neighbouring country, so that the cut across
country between the two forces looked as if it
might be an exciting one, though as long as the
lines were not actually cut I saw no reason why
we should not get through. All along our route
we never saw a sign of soldiers, either our own or
the enemy's, and eventually arrived at Roulers at
4.15 p.m., where I sought out the Corps Headquarters and reported myself.

1914.   I was ordered to proceed to Dunkerque, fill up
with ammunition, and go back that night.   At
Cortemarch we were held up for one and a half
hours, and only got as far as Dixmude by 11.30 p.m.
Here I was again held up, but was told that another
armoured train was coming from the west.   Guess-
ing that this would be Littlejohns with the 4·7-inch
Belgian section, I decided to await his arrival
before returning to Roulers; an hour later he
arrived, and we equalized our supplies of ammunition.   However, it took almost as long to return,
and it was 8 a.m. before we were all back at Roulers.

Oct. 14. There we found the Corps gone, but General
Capper had our orders.   Our troops were evacu-
ating Roulers, retiring to the high ground east of
Ypres, and we were detailed to protect their rear.

We left Roulers at 9.30 a.m. and shortly afterwards the Germans' patrol entered that town in
our rear.   By 3.30 p.m. the job was finished, so
Ypres. we moved on to Ypres Station and reported.
Whilst I was away on this errand, one of my
machinists sighted a stray Uhlan patrol, opened
fire with his rifle, and emptied two saddles.   We
saw a Taube shot down; the pilot was wearing
the Iron Cross, which decoration he had received
for being the first aviator to drop a bomb on
Antwerp.

Scattered firing could be heard from the direction of Mt. Kemmel, and we learnt that the cavalry

THE YPRES DISTRICT
showing
THE RAILWAY SYSTEM
SCALE

Railways ——— Roads ———
Canals ———

1914. of our main army had just taken the position—
one of great importance in the days to come.   It
was said that our 2nd Corps were advancing south
of us and had already occupied Armentières,
whilst our cavalry filled the gap between them
and ourselves, so that now we were back with Sir
John French's troops at last and held his left
flank.

That evening I had an excellent dinner in the
splendid little Hôtel de Châtelaine, a famous place
which fed us all for many days, the plucky pro-
prietor keeping it going till he was eventually
shelled out when the Germans gave vent to their
disappointed feelings at being unable to take the
town some two weeks later, and commenced their
systematic destruction of the main square, the
hotel itself being near-by the famous Cloth Hall
and Cathedral.   A great many of us have good
reason to bless this hotel-keeper's brave family.

Oct. 15th.   Early in the following morning I was sent out
to the Menin road-crossing to report to General
Houge Capper, whose Headquarters had been installed in
Château. the famous Houge Château.   There was nothing
doing during the day, for the enemy had not come
up with us, and we were busily engaged in selecting
our positions on the ridges.

During the afternoon my train was inspected by
Prince Arthur of Connaught.   In the evening I
got a message from Littlejohns saying he was

returning to Dunkerque, Boulogne, or Havre to 1914.
form a base for the trains.   Captain Servais left
with his train for another area, and Ridler had
gone to Boulogne to complete the armouring of
his two 6-inch gun bogies.

The next morning I was sent to the Frezemberg Oct. 16th.
Halte on the Roulers line, and from there on to
Zonnebeke to report to the Headquarters of the
22nd Brigade, where I had breakfast with General
Lawford and got a plan of our positions.   On our
extreme left our 3rd Cavalry Division was still
reconnoitring to the eastward of Passchendaele;
the 22nd Infantry Brigade were astride the Roulers
railway; the 21st to the Menin road; and the 20th
on our right when we were in touch with the
2nd Cavalry Division at Kortewilde.   Everywhere
things were very quiet, but all on our side were
extremely busy on their positions.   Returning to
the Menin crossing, I met General Capper, who
told me to go out on the Commes line and operate.
The Gordons were resting at this crossing and
were greatly amused at our quaint piece of artillery.
Arriving at Houthem, I found the Scots Greys
there, and from them obtained the details of the
hostile positions along the bank of the Lys from
Warneton to Bousbecque.

Moving on to a position at K. 23, I opened fire
with lyddite and shrapnel from all three guns on
various selected areas along these lines.   The

1914. country round here was absolutely flat and covered with trees, ditches, and isolated farms. The firing was quite blind, as no such thing as an observation post was possible; whilst aircraft spotting was still only being tried and no machines were available for us. Our advanced cavalry posts were in this position, but no enemy were seen, and at dusk we returned to Ypres.

Up till now the crews had been sleeping and living round their guns. Nights were getting cold, and the winter was at hand, so I obtained a guard's van and a couple of covered wagons from the railway authorities. In the former I made a cabin and office for myself in the " dicky " position used by the guard of a train, and built quarters for the petty officers in the body of the van. In a small timber-yard near the station we found a quantity of boarding and timber, from which each man was able to build billets for himself.

Their bunks were arranged three high all round, so that one wagon took eighteen men. Till now the train had been painted the Service grey, which was now the worse for wear, so I got a good supply of paint and brushes from the excellent *chef-de-gare*, and began painting the whole train in a camouflage design of yellow, green, and red, and before long we toned well with the autumnal colouring of the country around us.

By means of some telephones and wire I fitted

up telephonic communication between all three 1914.
guns and a centre position in the foremost magazine
wagon, which had an armoured ventilation hood
forming a most efficient conning tower in case of
close fighting. Thus I was able to control all the
guns on all round firing, except right astern. For
the normal shoots and bombardments I made out
all the orders from my cabin, where I had a suitable
table for maps, etc.

For any particular shoot the gunlayer was given
the details for his rounds on a chit of paper, but
when I could obtain the assistance of an observer,
I used the control position at the guns, for generally
the fighting sections—*i.e.*, the guns—were kept
some distance in front of the unprotected living
section, each section with its own engine. But
even now the arrangements at the guns themselves
were very primitive, and I badly required the
bearing arcs and a clinometer.

In the morning I was sent out again to Houthem Oct. 17th.
to repeat the firing of the previous day, but on
arrival there the Commander of the Greys objected,
for he said he had located hostile batteries at
Comines, and if I opened fire I should draw a return
fire upon his neighbourhood. This put me in a
quandary, for mine were Corps orders, but I
obeyed the man on the spot and returned to Ypres
to tell them so. They agreed to this and sent me
out to Zonnebeke instead, to be at the disposal

4

1914. of the Brigade there, but throughout the day things continued to be very quiet.

That evening I had a hot bath, the first decent scrub since leaving England. Whilst at Houthem that morning Lieutenant ff.-Blake came on board; we had been shipmates in the old *Britannia* days, but he left us and joined the Cavalry. He produced a German lance, which we erected on the top of my van and flew our ensign from it. I had bought the silk at Ypres and one of the men sewed it together.

That night the orders were issued for the advance, which was to take place next day, when we were to move towards Menin—that town famous for its leaf tobacco manufacture, of which the quantity put forth was out of all proportion to its quality of doubtful fragrancy.* Though little did we realize that we should be moving forward in the face of numerous hostile formations

120,000 the presence of which had not yet been felt. We against 20,000. were soon to discover, however, that descending upon us was the full weight of three German Army Corps, the 23rd, 26th, and 27th. Our noble 7th Division were about to bump up against a force hopelessly outnumbering it by six to one.

Throughout that night various additional orders arrived, and by 3 a.m. I had orders to be in two different places in the morning; however, I got

* See Appendix I.

this settled by the Division, and by 5 a.m. got 1914.
definite orders to act as General Capper himself
wished.

At 6 a.m. I took up a position near Houthem Oct. 18.
and opened fire on Gheluwe. The Cavalry asked
me to knock out a farm about 1,500 yards down   An
the line, where they declared the Germans had towards
                                                 Menin.
posted a machine gun which had already caused
us some casualties. Leaving two guns in action
on Gheluwe, I tried the other one, but the telephone wires were in the way, and a trial shot only
missed over and hit the village of Comines beyond.
However, I tried with the 6-pounder, and after
exploding a few shell on the wires and posts,
eventually blew a clear range through the wires
and got on to the farm. After a few rounds we
steamed out towards it, but everything was very
quiet, and if the Germans had been there before
they certainly were not there now. From a
hundred yards we put a few more shells into the
neighbouring outhouses to make it certain, and
then returned to the main train and rejoined in
the work there. For some time this continued,
also firing on Wervicq and Menin areas, and shortly
after 9 a.m. I was informed that so far our advance
had progressed and that our men were just east
of Trehand—an advance of quite two miles.
Meanwhile I had shifted position 200 yards back,
for it was not wise to remain firing in one spot

1914. for too long; and, sure enough, at 9.40 a.m. a hostile battery opened fire, four high-explosive shells bursting on the metals in the position vacated.

This caused some misgivings to the local cavalry Commander, who asked me to move farther away still, so as to leave his area as clear as possible. I went back as far as K. 25, near Hollebeke, and continued firing on the Wervicq sector, and then back still farther to K. 27 and opened fire on Comines, which lay clearly in view before us. If it was any consolation to the cavalry in front of me, this succeeded in drawing the shell-fire back from them upon ourselves, for again we got shelled, but quite harmlessly.

The noise of battle gradually quietened and eventually ceased, so I returned and reported, being sent on to Poperinghe to report to the Corps. There General Rawlinson wanted to know where Littlejohns was with his other train, but I could only show him the vague information I possessed on that point. I had to wait there till the orders for the continuance of the advance were issued for the morrow.

During the day our 3rd Cavalry had been able to wheel round on our left and were at St. Pieter, and our line ran south-east from there to Houthem. My orders arrived at 10 p.m. and also the plans for the next day. So far we had not run up against any exceptionally hard obstacles, so were

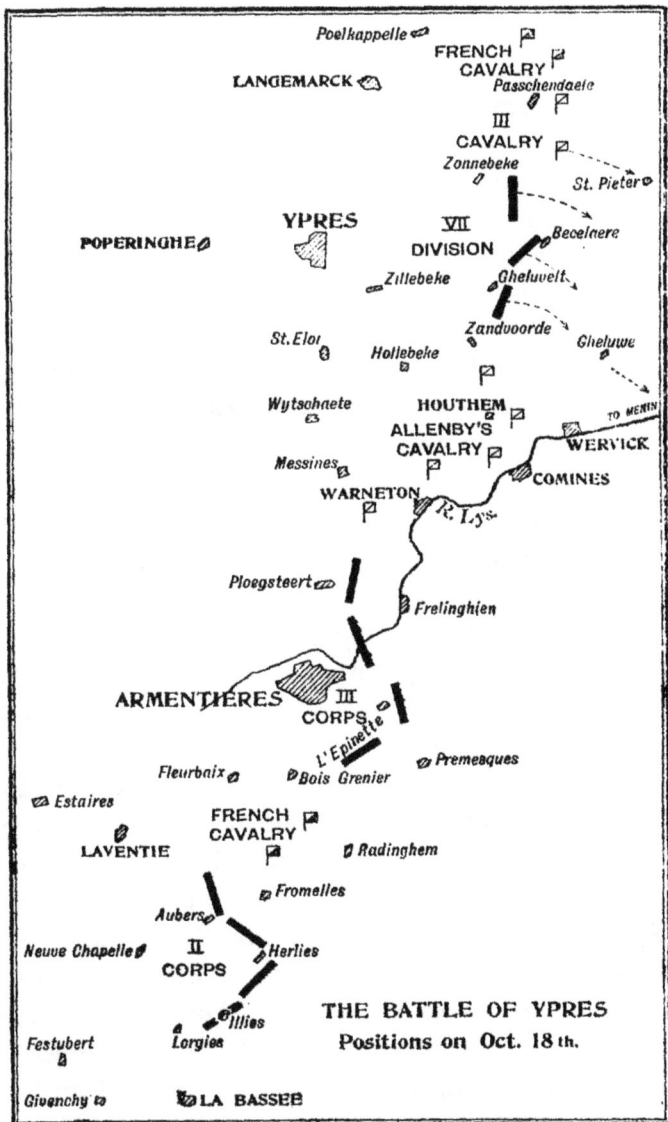

Poelkappelle

LANGEMARCK

FRENCH
CAVALRY

Passchendaele

III
CAVALRY

Zonnebeke

St. Pieter

YPRES

VII
DIVISION

Becelaere

POPERINGHE

Zillebeke

Gheluvelt

Zandvoorde

Gheluwe

St. Elot

Hollebeke

Wytschaete

HOUTHEM
ALLENBY'S
CAVALRY

Messines

WARNETON

TO MENIN

WERVICK

COMINES

R. Lys.

Ploegsteert

Frelinghien

ARMENTIERES

III
CORPS

L'Epinette

Bois Grenier

Premesques

Fleurbaix

Estaires

FRENCH
CAVALRY

Radinghem

LAVENTIE

Fromelles

Aubers

Neuve Chapelle

II
CORPS

Herlies

THE BATTLE OF YPRES
Positions on Oct. 18 th.

Illies

Festubert

Lorgies

Givenchy to

LA BASSEE

1914. to take Klephoek and Gheluwe, and then follow up by occupying Menin, and thus the whole northern bank of the Lys, supported by the 2nd Cavalry on our right.

Oct. 19. By dawn I was already in position at Houthem, where I had been directed to fire from, but this again disturbed the cavalry, whose horses were all sheltering in the village, so I moved back again

The Attack on Menin. to K. 26. Orders to commence the attack reached me at 9.10 a.m., when I began the bombardment of the hostile positions at Wervicq. During the forenoon Littlejohns arrived with the Belgian section and joined in the firing after I had explained what was wanted to him.

Further orders were expected, for I had already received a warning to be ready to rush round viâ Roulers and join up with our left flank; however, none arrived, though very heavy firing continued up in that direction.

Early in the afternoon orders arrived for us to go to Zonnebeke, but when we reached there things did not seem very disturbed, and no further orders arrived till dusk, when we returned to Ypres, where we learnt that our attack had been stopped, and that we had begun to feel the pressure of the huge forces against us. During the fore-noon our 3rd Cavalry on our left had been pressed in from the north, and in the end the whole Division had to slowly retrace its steps, fighting all the

way, till they reached their original positions of 1914.
the previous morning.

The pressure on the north was increasing and
things began to look dark, though our hopes were
raised by the news that General Haig with his
1st Corps was coming up from the Aisne to our
assistance.   Next morning we were out again, and Oct 20th.
went to Zonnebeke to assist our cavalry on the
left, who were already as far back as Passchendaele-
Keiberg.   Our first objectives were the approaches
to Moorslede, upon which all guns were turned.
Later a message arrived that the French cavalry
had been forced out of Passchendaele, and that
we were to fire upon that village.

About noon orders came to open fire upon
hostile infantry which were seen advancing from
Keiberg, so we opened fire on that area, and from
then on throughout the whole afternoon various
orders continued to arrive, so that we had a busy
time of it.

First Broodseinde—right in front of us—then
Passchendaele, Goldberg, Passchendaele again,
Nieuwemolen, and once again Passchendaele.   All
these places in turn were our targets—a call for
help here, assistance ordered there, and so on—
all hard to miss; the last we could see burning
furiously.   Though at first a novelty, it is easy
to quickly tire of burning villages and of destroying the homes of our Ally, and even of firing away

1914. into the *blue* at the enemy and his positions, yet it was little bits of consideration such as the following, which arrived after a bombardment of Passchendaele, that go far to relieve the monotony and to invigorate the spirit:

From G.O.C. 5th French Cavalry.

"The effect of your fire appears to have produced a most excellent res·lt against the attack of the enemy, and we thank you for your able support."

That night after we all had returned to Ypres Littlejohns left for the Yser front to join up with the Belgians there.   Out again at dawn I went to Zonnebeke under the orders of the 22nd Brigade, who gave me a battery east of Broodseinde as the first target; and upon this we began a searching fire.   All round shells of various calibres were flying and exploding in any place, aimed at nothing in particular apparently, and certainly the very great majority did no more than plough into the earth harmlessly; but in front, all along the ridge, shelling and rifle-fire showed where the two forces met and where the heavy fighting was taking place.

My firing at the battery was quite indirect, for the ridge and woods hid everything to the east except a few prominent villages and spires, etc.

Later in the morning a message arrived saying that our left had been pressed back, so I retreated

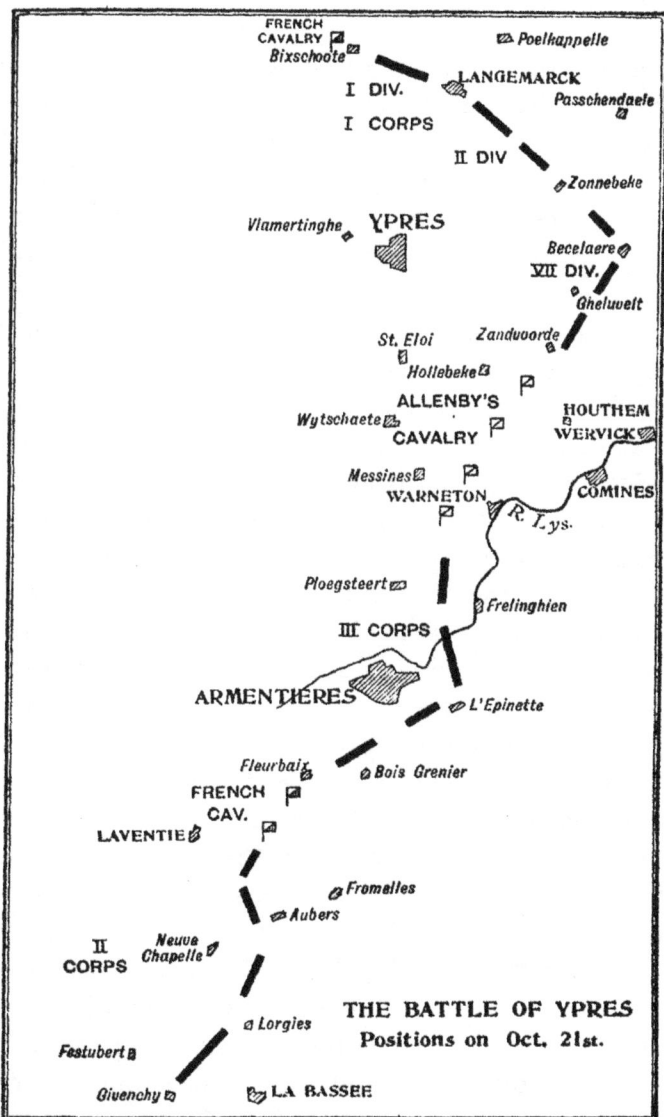

FRENCH
CAVALRY
Bixschoote
Poelkappelle
LANGEMARCK
I DIV.
I CORPS
Passchendaele
II DIV
Zonnebeke
Vlamertinghe
YPRES
Becelaere
VII DIV.
Gheluvelt
St. Eloi
Zandvoorde
Hollebeke
ALLENBY'S
HOUTHEM
Wytschaete
CAVALRY
WERVICK
Messines
COMINES
WARNETON
R. Lys.
Ploegsteert
Frelinghien
III CORPS
ARMENTIÈRES
L'Epinette
Fleurbaix
Bois Grenier
FRENCH
CAV.
LAVENTIE
Fromelles
Aubers
II
CORPS
Neuve
Chapelle
Lorgies
THE BATTLE OF YPRES
Positions on Oct. 21st.
Festubert
Givenchy
LA BASSEE

behind the Ypres road to K. 8, and from there
opened fire on Passchendaele once more. This
continued to be my target up till noon, when I
was sent back to Ypres and out to Boesinghe,
there to report to the 1st Division—General Lomax.
This was the first I had heard of the actual arrival
of the 1st Corps, and their arrival must have
cheered up everyone, for the menace on our flank
looked very black.

By 2 p.m. I had found the Headquarters, and
was directed to go out and shell Poelcapelle, from
which direction our troops were being hard pressed.
It seemed that during the forenoon the Divisions
had started their advance as soon as they had
arrived on the field with the idea of forcing the
enemy back towards Bruges, but after an initial
success they were very soon brought to a stop by
masses of the enemy and intense artillery fire.
At 4 a.m. my objective was changed to the station
itself, which would be visible if I advanced a few
hundred yards. This I did and opened a direct
fire on it at 2,000 yards, so that it was soon in
flames. Wallemollem also was given me as a
target, so I opened on this as well.

Half an hour after this was begun, I noticed a
mounted officer dashing up to us, who when he
arrived said that the French cavalry on our left
had been driven in, and that the Germans were
500 yards on my left flank. A quick retreat

seemed advisable, so I ran back to K. 46 and 1914.
continued firing from there, for I did not relish
the idea of finding the Huns too close behind me.
However, the French were soon rallied and able to
hold back the threat.   At dusk I returned to the
Headquarters and then on to Ypres for the night.

The following morning I was again sent to join Oct. 22nd.
the 22nd Brigade and ran out to Zonnebeke, but
at the Ypres road crossing I found the Warwicks
busily engaged in digging reserve trenches, so that
after a few hasty words I retreated to a less
prominent position at Frezemberg Halte.   The
Warwicks told us of the awful shelling they had
experienced during the night, and indeed, poor
fellows ! they looked as if they had been through
everything.

I learnt the whereabouts of the new Brigade
Headquarters, for their old quarters in Zonnebeke
was now a pile of bricks and dust, and set out to
find them.   On the way I met the remnants of the
1st Welsh Fusiliers—6 officers and 300 men; the
others had fallen during the last few days in the
awful fighting, but most of them during yesterday's and last night's shelling.   Early in the
afternoon we opened fire on Becelaere and Gheluvelt, but had not been long on this job when orders
arrived for me to report to the 3rd Cavalry, who
had now moved round to the right flank of the
7th Division and were in the line at Zandvoorde.

1914. I found General Byng at his temporary headquarters at Klein-Zillebeke and then got more
precise details of the positions in the sector. My
first target was Houthem, which was in full view
after moving out as far as Hollebeke. The range
was 3,000 yards, so that the effect of the T.N.T.
upon the unfortunate houses and roads was most
brilliant for our forty-five minutes' bombardment.
Various members of the cavalry force came on
board and were very loud in their praise of the
effect of our shell, which firing they had watched
during the shelling on Passchendaele in front of
them when they held that sector; it was something
to know that we were doing good, for if it was so
then, why not generally ? That evening I had
to report to the 4th Corps at Ypres. For the last
two days I had sent various telegrams off to the
base for more ammunition, because our supply
was direct from England to ourselves viâ Dunkerque instead of through the Army channels, which
would have been much more convenient; now I
had only sufficient left for one day's heavy shoot.
Each evening we had to return to Ypres to clean
fires, and fill up with fuel and water, for the engines
had now been under constant steam for three
weeks, and only careful nursing would keep them
in perfect order.

23rd. Early in the morning I was out again under the
3rd Cavalry, and went forward to continue the

bombardment of Houlthem. Firing was going on
all along the line, and it was obvious that hard
fighting was in progress. This Cavalry Division
was on the right of the 20th Brigade, who were
being heavily shelled, and occupied the line between
Zandvoorde and round Kortewilde. Various types
of shell were flying around, and the roads were a
certain target of shrapnel. So I opened a direct
fire on the roofs, etc., of Houthem, and soon got
back a reply from some battery concealed on the
left of the line, but it got no nearer than bursting
high shrapnel overhead. It seemed as if its con-
cealment stopped it bringing a direct fire upon us;
however, it was eventually located an hour later,
when I turned on to them.

About 1.30 p.m. more precise details of the
hostile trenches and gun positions were sent to me,
so I sent a messenger to ask if I could run out
along the line and get a direct fire at them, but
the General said he thought it too risky in view of
the prevailing uncertainty ahead. All this time
shrapnel was bursting on our left in the trees and
shells were falling around in all directions, but
from the hundreds which fell, extremely few did
any harm, due to this form of unobserved firing.
Throughout the whole afternoon we were engaged
continuously on any of six different targets to the
south-eastward, and at last towards dusk came to
the limit of my supplies—a sad state, which I

1914. reported to the Headquarters, and then returned
to Ypres to see if a replenishment had arrived.

Telegrams brought no reply, and by the following forenoon I was exasperated and in perplexity
as to what to do. At last at 11 a.m. I got news
that a 6-inch gun with trucks of ammunition and
stores had left Boulogne, and was told to go to
Hazebrouck to meet them. I reported this to the
Corps, and by 11.25 got away, arriving there at
1 p.m. From there we were sent to St. Omer,
but nothing was known there of my quarry. At
this time General Headquarters were in this town,
so I sought out the Director of Transport, through
whom I got the news that such a gun and wagons
had been seen shunting about Boulogne during
the forenoon, and again, later, further news that
they had left attached to a train at 11 a.m. It
was not till 8 p.m. that the train arrived, bringing
me 300 rounds for my 4·7 guns and a 6-inch gun
which was now armoured and provided with a
quantity of its own ammunition. But just as we
were about to go east again, orders arrived that I
was to remain at St. Omer. Meanwhile I had sent
the engines into the sheds for their much-needed
cleaning.

That evening the following communication was
received, as it was to be communicated to all
troops from the Field-Marshal Commander-in-
Chief:

" *23rd October,* 1914.

" The Field-Marshal Commanding-in-Chief wishes 1914. once more to make known to his troops how deeply he appreciates the bravery and endurance which they have displayed since their arrival in the northern theatre. In circulating the official information which records the splendid victories of our Russian Allies, he would remind the troops that the enemy must before long withdraw troops to the East and relieve the tension on our front, and he feels it quite unnecessary to urge officers and men to make a determined effort and drive the enemy over the frontier."

Towards noon next day we got orders to proceed again to Ypres, at which place we arrived by 4 p.m., when I reported to the 4th Corps. However, General Rawlinson told me that now the armoured trains had been taken over by the General Headquarters, and that he must get instructions from them before he could give me orders to work under him; meanwhile I was to wait in Ypres. At 3 a.m. I was rung up by the Corps Chief-of-Staff, Oct. 26th. General Montgomery, who asked me to go out in the early morning on his responsibility and engage the guns at " America," for they were causing great trouble to the 20th Brigade holding Kruiseecke. By dawn I was in position at K. 27 on the Comines line and opened fire on the area indicated.

About 8 a.m. the Germans began a violent shelling of Hollebeke on my left, and started

1914. making a dead set at the church, which, from our
point of view on the flank, made a most picturesque
bit of shooting. They first ranged on the church
with high explosive, and then burst into salvos
of shrapnel. After first straddling the roof with
a line of high bursts, they next hit, then never
missing, the roof and building, so that within a
few minutes it was in flames.

In time our turn came, and someone directed
his attention on to our position, for we were
straddled three times in succession, after which I
withdrew round the bend and into the shelter of
the woods for a while, where at 10.30 a.m. I got
orders to return to Ypres. The station was occupied by hospital trains and a train of trucks
filled with German prisoners, who were being
despatched in large numbers. The Red Cross
Sisters came on board and told us that they had
first heard of us from the wounded German
prisoners, who had told them that our presence
was well known to them and that we were very
much disliked; also, that a hot time was in store
for us if we were caught, for their Emperor had
offered £1,000 for our capture.* Naturally we felt
something proud, but as equally determined that
he was to be disappointed and perhaps inclined to
raise the price.

Whilst at the Corps Headquarters I had a look

* See Appendix III.

GERMAN PRISONERS AT YPRES.

To face page 64.

at a large crowd of Germans who were assembled 1914·
in the famous Cloth Hall.   Such a motley crowd
in that fine building looked very out of place, for
they were going through a process of search and
interrogation.   Everything except their clothes
and personal belongings was collected in.

During the preceding day the Germans had
found the exact range of our lines around
Kruiseecke, and their defenders had been going
through the same awful experience as their comrades of the 22nd Brigade some days before.
They—the 20th Brigade—had been attacked all
day long and during the night, and after their
trenches had been blown to bits they had to
abandon the position and take up another line
between Zandevoorde and Gheluvelt, the Brigadier
being wounded and the remnants of the Brigade
itself relieved and withdrawn.

At 2 p.m. orders came to go out and fire again
on the "America" positions and on Kolenberg;
twenty minutes later we were in action again.

Fighting could be seen to be in progress in front
of us at Kortewilde, and on our right at Hollebeke.
Some of our troops were passing under the bridge
beneath us and forming up in open order in front
of us abreast the Hollebeke Château, and were
advancing towards Kortewilde as if they were at
drill.   Meanwhile shells and shrapnel were flying
all round.   During the firing on our targets a note

5

1914. arrived signed by " Scottie "; whoever he was I never found out, but he wanted a certain trench shelled, the position of which was 1,000 yards just in front of us. Keeping everyone behind the armour, I took one of the guns out and at 600 yards range opened fire with the 6-pounder. The railway was so highly banked that the 4·7-inch guns could not depress enough, so we had to stand up in the open and use the 6-pounder anti-aircraft gun.

Our own line of trenches was quite noticeable, for at every round fired khaki heads kept popping up to see either if we were still there aiming at them or at the Boche, but probably they were as anxious about their own heads as I was, for owing to the very short distance separating the two lines and the flat trajectory of the shell at such short range the projectile could only have been missing them by a few feet overhead. A quarter of an hour was long enough as we were in full view of the enemy and might at any moment become a point-blank target for some gun if I stopped, so I retreated to the remainder of the train. I hoped that if we did not do all that the troops hoped for or expected, at any rate we put up a small show for their amusement which varied the monotony of their day.*

That evening when I returned to report I got orders to proceed to Bethune with the 4·7 guns

* See Appendix II.

and join the 2nd Corps, and that Ridler was coming 1914 up with his other 6-inch gun and so form his train. Naturally I was very loth to leave this field of operations, but was consoled with the knowledge that things were just as lively at the right as on this the left flank of the battle.

That evening we left at 10.25 p.m. and arrived at Bethune at 4 a.m.

The following are extracts from the Corps Bulletin:

" In the diaries of captured German officers the most unreserved compliments are paid to the shooting both of our infantry and our artillery. Our guns, they say, drop their shells with such marvellous accuracy on the target that there is only a yard or two between one shot and the next. One officer wonders whether we locate our targets mainly by means of our aircraft, which, he says, are always flying over their troops, or whether we are in telephonic communication with observers behind their own lines.

" As for our infantry, he remarked that our fellows ' shoot extraordinarily well '; as soon as a head shows above the trenches bullets begin to whistle past. On one occasion the Germans found themselves under a deadly fire, when they were near the village of Koelborg, but at a considerable distance from our trenches. So sure were they that the bullets could not come from us that they set fire to the village as a punishment for supposed franc-tireurs, who, in fact, did not exist. A

1914 compliment to us, but rather rough on the villagers.

" An officer captured the other day by the 7th Division has a sufficiently extraordinary tale to tell. In the course of our advance he found himself left with about twenty men in a house within our lines. He stayed there for three days before he was discovered and made prisoner. The moral is that the fact of a building being within our lines does not prove that it harbours none of the enemy.

" Amongst the enormous and varied booty captured by the Russians in the brilliant victory is the German Crown Prince's car containing his own most personal belongings. There is a rumour, so far lacking confirmation, that in order to facilitate their rapid retirement before the Russians when the roads are blocked with their own fleeing troops, the German Commanders and Princes are in future to be provided with Zeppelins.

" The following dreadful doggerel is a fairly close translation of a war song found on a prisoner. It was not possible from an inspection of the printed copy to determine whether the owner had sung it often, but it is surmised that after the retreat from the Marne the ditty has not been rendered with the confident abandon that marked the earlier concerts of the campaign.

" (For a proper understanding of the song it must be remembered that the Landwehr consists of men between the ages of twenty-seven and thirty-nine who have served their two or three years with the colours, and then four or five years in the reserve; they are liable to a maximum of

twenty-eight days' training between the ages of 1914.
twenty-seven and thirty-two, but are not called
up for training afterwards.)

" ' A SONG OF WAR.

*(First sung by the 4th Co., 1st Batt. 106th Landwehr Regt.,
24th Division, 19th Army Corps. Composed by Lieut.
Kotzsch. Tune—" The Vicar of Bray sur Somme.")*

> Hi ! Nicholas, my pretty chit,
> Take my advice and hop it ! Git !
> We've just begun to stretch our legs;
> We'll catch you sure as eggs is eggs—
> > We Landwehr,
> > Ho ! Landwehr,
> The blithely carolling Landwehr.
>
> You too, you tiny President,
> You're getting too impertinent;
> If you don't mend your manners quick,
> We'll dust your breeks the same as Nick—
> > We Landwehr,
> > Yah ! Landwehr,
> The stamping, ramping Landwehr.
>
> And you, King George, whom nothing shames,
> We'll soon be sailing up your Thames,
> Making a truly German noise,
> For we're the Kaiser's bonniest boys,
> > We Landwehr,
> > Rah ! Landwehr.
> The howling, scowling Landwehr.
>
> So off together, brawlers three,
> Unless you want to taste the Spree;
> But ere you do your triple scoot
> You'll feel the Landwehr's hefty boot
> > Just land where
> > The Landwehr
> In early boyhood tanned were.

Peter, you knave, in Servian sty,
Franz-Joseph comes to wipe your eye;
No need to pray on bended knees,
We listen to no weakling's pleas—
　　　　We Landwehr,
　　　　Yes, Landwehr,
The dashing, slashing Landwehr.

Sing, Austrian brother, jodel, shout,
The German Landwehr pulls you out,
Surely you hear our Battle Call
" Kaiser and Country," and ('bove all)
　　　　The Landwehr,
　　　　Ho ! Landwehr,
The God's Own Chosen Landwehr.' "

II.—Givenchy.

On arriving at Bethune, I received a message to
return to Hazebrouck and intercept Ridler, who
had more ammunition and some stores for us. I
had not seen him since I left them all at Ostend
on the 10th, and all this time he had been forced
to remain at the base completing his train, and
naturally was very eager to go out and begin work
with his two 6-inch. I was back again in Bethune,
by 11 a.m. and sent on to Beuvry Station to report
to the 5th Division there—General Morland.

By the time I found the Headquarters and got
the maps and details of the positions it was already
dark, so I got the orders for the next day and
returned to Bethune, where there was at last a
decent engine workshop which my engines could
use. A hot fight was in progress at Neuve Chapelle,

the remains of which village eventually were left
in the fringe of the German lines a few days later.
The Lahore Division under General Willcocks was
in the neighbourhood in support, so that all around
us we met these big Indian soldiers. Most of the
batteries were using telephonic communication
with their observers in front, but that was as yet
beyond me; however, I was to have the assistance
of an aeroplane to spot for me. Verey coloured
lights were used for a code to indicate the fall of
shot.

On arrival at Beuvry next morning at dawn I
found that all the points were locked to foul, and
as there were no authorities at the deserted station
I had to smash the padlocks to pass through. I
ran out to a position about 1,000 yards west of
Cuinchy Station and proceeded to clear the poles
and telephone wires out of the way, for they ran
along the northern side of the lines and thus were
foul of my guns. This took much time, for the
wires had to be kept clear, some of them being
used to form part of the signal system between the
posts in front and the positions in rear. My orders
were to engage two particular batteries at Voilaines
until the airman arrived, and then to use him for
spotting. By 9 a.m. I was ready and commenced
firing. A French battery of 75's just on my left
were somewhat surprised at my curious form of
artillery.

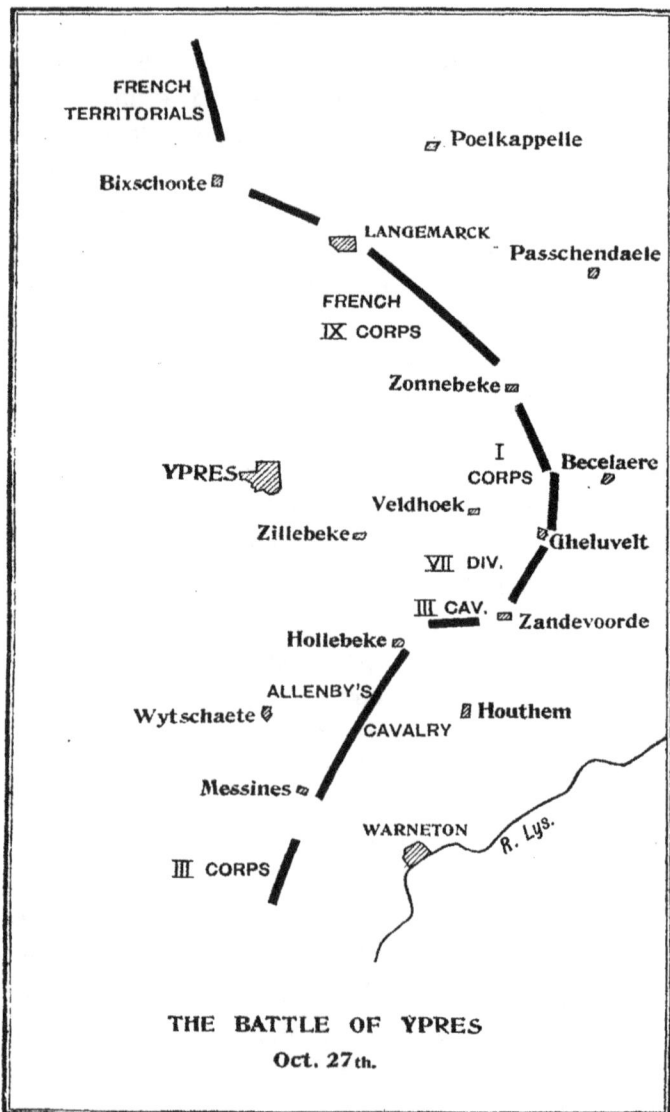

FRENCH
TERRITORIALS

Poelkappelle

Bixschoote

LANGEMARCK

Passchendaele

FRENCH
IX CORPS

Zonnebeke

I
CORPS

Becelaere

YPRES

Veldhoek

Zillebeke

Gheluvelt

VII DIV.

III CAV.

Zandevoorde

Hollebeke

ALLENBY'S

Wytschaete

Houthem

CAVALRY

Messines

WARNETON

R. Lys.

III CORPS

THE BATTLE OF YPRES
Oct. 27th.

In this locality again direct firing was out of the 1914.
question, for the ridge in front and the village of
Givenchy and Cuinchy filled the horizon, though
the steeples of La Bassée and Douvrin Churches
were outstanding on the skyline. But we were a
bit better off here than at Ypres, for the maps
showed every house, and it was possible to lay
for a particular spot on the skyline on a bearing
in line with the actual target beyond.

At midday the airman arrived overhead to
co-operate with us. He signalled the first salvo
as falling to the right and next as line correct.
For some reason he now sailed home again, so I
continued firing on this line for an hour. Meanwhile he had landed and sent me a message saying
that we were just too far over the target, but all
the shell were landing into the village itself, which
we had put in flames—a fact which Headquarters
were not displeased with, for they said that
damage to persons and material must have
resulted.

We were to try again, but the airman broke his
propeller on leaving the ground and did not arrive
again till 3.30 p.m. At first he had some difficulty
in spotting the lyddite in the broken country, but
eventually we got line and range correct, continuing on this target till dusk. When he landed,
the airman sent a report that when he left we were
straddling the right-hand gun of the hostile battery,

1914. so that there was little doubt that we were warming
them up, to say the least of it.

During this afternoon the French General Commandant of the 116th Brigade had sent me details
of his positions in front of Givenchy, and requested that I should tell him what he could do to
give me his most complete co-operation. This
Brigade was on the right flank of our 2nd Corps,
and was thus the connecting-link between the
two national armies. That evening I returned to
Bethune.

Oct. 29th.   My orders for the next day were to wait out in
position ready to continue with the airman when
he arrived. However, the morning was very
foggy and there seemed no early chance of making
a start. Meanwhile heavy shelling and much
rifle-fire was going on in front at Givenchy and
to the north, shells were flying round in various
odd fields and spent bullets continued to buzz
about, some of them flattening out on our armour.
I learnt that an attack was being made by the
enemy, and that they had entered our trenches
held by the Manchesters.

The airman must have reported on the impossibility of his co-operation, for at 8.10 a.m. I was
told to carry on independently as yesterday; so
that we again opened fire on the Voilaines batteries;
this firing and the buzzing ricochets from the fighting
going on in front kept us busy during the forenoon.

THE TRAIN BEHIND GIVENCHY.

To face page 74.

About midday the following message arrived 1914·
from Headquarters:

To 108th, 114th, 2nd Siege, and Armoured Train.
" Airman reports that at least three batteries
have evacuated their positions since yesterday.
He is not sure about two others. The G.O.C.
congratulates you on your excellent shooting."

This was a very encouraging beginning. By
4 p.m. the fog had reduced so little in density
that the day's original programme seemed doomed
to be a wash-out, so I opened fire on an area at
" les 3 maisons," where a large crowd of wagons
and horses were congregated, and at dusk returned
to report.

We were out again early and waiting for fresh Oct. 30th.
orders. Reports stated that our bivouac target
of last night had disappeared, so we must have
moved that lot, and soon directions to search the
Voilaines positions arrived. Whilst engaged on
this firing the French Brigade asked me to destroy
a house 200 yards in front of their own troops at
Givenchy, but I could not do this, for what with
the uncertainty of indirect laying and having no
observation, it seemed almost as likely that I
should hit the French as the house; moreover, I
had my own work to do. That evening I was
told that an airman had reported our shell were
falling round the position of the battery—our

1914. target, also that the 2nd Corps were being relieved by the Meerut Division, General Willcocks; the former was practically in a state of complete physical exhaustion owing to the want of sleep and incessant labours during the past weeks, and the dreadful thinning of their ranks. This sort of warfare with unseen enemies and big explosions would be new to these Indian warriors, but it was hoped they would get used to it, as, indeed, they soon did after the first few experiences, which resulted in unnecessary loss due to their imprudent gallantry.

Oct. 31st.   All the next forenoon we were busy on the Voilaines positions, whilst more fighting was going on at Givenchy. The French informed me that they had attacked and had succeeded in advancing as far as the western apex of the triangular system of railway-lines, a small part of France which was going to play an important part in our winter campaign in the near future. That night I was ordered to return to Boulogne to refit the train.

Refitting at Boulogne.   Accordingly we left Bethune, arriving at Boulogne at 4 a.m., where I had my second hot bath since leaving England and at last slept in a bed. I found Littlejohns and reported. He had an office in the Métropole, from which he controlled the three trains.

Some weeks before it had been decided to give each train a distinguishing name, and I had chosen the name of the C.-in-C. of our Grand Fleet for 1914. mine; now our cap ribbons had arrived, and every man wore " H.M.A.T. Jellicoe " on his cap.

I took the train into the repair yard and had the guns lifted out so as to get at the mountings for complete overhaul. Proper large bearing arcs were engraved and fitted to each mounting, and after a certain amount of argument I got a clinometer from England. Our living quarters were decently and more comfortably fitted out, and a small cooking-stove was purchased for each wagon, whilst an additional truck was secured and fitted up as a storeroom. The camouflaging was done up and each gun wagon given a name, those of our famous Admirals—Drake, Howe, and Nelson— being selected.

By November 7th we were ready again for service, but Littlejohns went to London and I remained in Boulogne to take charge of the base in his place. During this period Boulogne was a very sad spectacle, for it was filled with our wounded who continually streamed in from the terrible battle raging all along our front and especially at Ypres. Everywhere hospitals had been started and were full; as fast as they were cleared into hospital ships, they were filled again from more trains from the east.

On November 11th Ridler sent a message to say that his train had met with an accident, a derail-

ment having caused a certain amount of damage
which put his unit out of action. Littlejohns
returned from England and said that our shell
supply ought to be at Dunkerque. The next day
I received orders to go to Ypres, so arranged to go
to Dunkerque first to see if our ammunition was
there, and if so to fill up. This course was approved and we got away the same night, but an
accident forced us to go viâ Calais, St. Omer, and
Hazebrouck. However, we arrived at 9.30 a.m.
and found the shell. At the same time we were
able to fill our provision wagon with various
food-stuffs from the Naval Division stores, which
were still there; this supply of luxuries, such as
tinned salmon, marmalade, sugar, milk, cheese,
and rum, was a great blessing during the winter
months to come.

III.—YPRES AGAIN.

We eventually got a clear route again that
evening and arrived the same night at Poperinghe,
where I found the Headquarters of the 1st Corps,
whose Artillery Chief, General Horne, now was
my Commander. I found there one of Ridler's
6-inch guns which had not been damaged in the
accident, and this was attached to my train with
a third engine. Ridler himself took the remainder
of his unit off to Boulogne for repairs. In re-
arranging the train I put the 6-inch behind the

IN ACTION AT YPRES.

To face page 78.

4·7 section, so that when going out to action I 1914. could keep the two calibres separated, and where possible on opposite pairs of rails. All joined together we made a big and heavy train, and much too big a target in an advanced position; the living-wagons with their engine were always kept well in the rear.

From the Headquarters I got the details of the positions and a short summary of recent events. When I left the front a fortnight before, the battle was spread out all along the line; lately it had very much bunched up in this particular sector.

The French 9th Corps were on the right. Our Ypres once more. 1st Corps were holding the line from Reutel round the edge of Polygon Wood to Veldhoek, and a large salient round Hill 60, as far as the Comines Canal, where we joined the French 16th Corps.

On the 11th the 1st Corps had held up a terrific attack, and yesterday it had been the French turn; the two armies still held their ground. Some time before, the Germans had commenced destroying Ypres with guns of all calibres, in brutal vengeance at being defeated in their efforts to break through. I was told that the station at Ypres had especially suffered and would need some reconnoitring before I could use it, which I did on the following day, finding that there still remained one complete line through the station, though the other six had been destroyed. As luck would have it, the complete line was a siding running on the southern side and nearest to the Germans, whose shells going over it just missed.

My targets consisted of six different battery positions to choose from for daylight firing, and certain areas which were probable places of assembly of supply and relief columns to be bombarded each evening at dusk. At dark I was to return and report at Headquarters. During the afternoon we passed through Ypres and took up a position at K. 2 on the Roulers line, opening fire at 3.45 on three different batteries with both calibres for forty-five minutes, repeating the firing at 4.30 p.m. At dusk we carried out the evening's programme of bombardments and then returned to Poperinghe. All day long snow and sleet had been falling.

I found that there was only one and a half miles of clear run on the Roulers line and of two on the Comines line, which I could use so long as the way through Ypres remained unbroken. If that was smashed beyond repair I would have to resort to the Boesinghe line and fire over Ypres itself, for the main line to Poperinghe was too close to our own main roads of communication, upon which it would not be wise to draw fire.

We were well provided for in the matter of " food," for in addition to our own stock on board we drew rations and bread from the A.S.C. More-

over, to the east of Ypres were a number of deserted 1914.
plots where some vegetables continued to grow,
from which we were able to draw an occasional
supply.   I have also recollections of an occasional
chicken getting run over, and being subsequently
cooked.   The following menu for a day is a standard of our living:

Daylight ..	..	Cup of tabloid tea.
Breakfast, 8.30 a.m.	..	Army rasher and fried bread; tinned butter; marmalade; tabloid tea.
Dinner, noon ..	..	Tinned rabbit; cheese and bread; rum.
Tea, 4 p.m. ..	..	Tea; bread and jam.
Supper, 8 p.m.	..	Bovril tabloid; beef and a vegetable; bread and jam; tea.

Daily Menu.

The beef and rabbits were sometimes varied Nov. 16th.
according to circumstances by tinned salmon or
the proceeds of a farmyard accident.

That night we received the sad news of the death
of Earl Roberts.

Early next morning the congested traffic between
Vlamertinghe and Poperinghe held us up, so that
we did not get clear before noon.   The shelling of
Ypres was in progress, and in view of the chance
of having the lines cut behind me, I decided to
remain west of Ypres except when actually going
to carry out a shoot.

6

1914.   Firing orders arrived in the early afternoon, so
we went to the same spot as yesterday and opened
fire, the 6-inch engaging a battery at Zandevoorde
and the 4·7's a battery near Hollebeke. This
firing continued at intervals during the afternoon
until it was time to repeat the evening's programme.
Zillebeke and the area in front of us was getting
a good shelling from both big and small guns,
whilst the shells fired at Ypres passed shrieking
over our heads. At one time a few salvos of large
stuff, about 8·2-inch, fell too close to us, one
75 yards short of the metals, making a huge hole
measuring 6 yards in diameter and 15 feet
deep.

It had been a miserable day, for rain had fallen
on and off all the time. That night I got permission to use Vlamertinghe as a base and so be
clear of the traffic. I could obtain water from
there for the engines, and used one of them alter-
nately to run me to Poperinghe each night, and
, whilst I was away reporting, the engine filled up
with fuel. Surprising to say, the water service
at Ypres Station was still intact, so that on peaceful
occasions we could fill up there when passing
through.

Nov 17th.   Next morning was even worse, for it was blowing
as well as raining, but we went east and opened
fire at 9.30 a.m. on three different targets. However, we had hardly warmed up to the work, when

6-INCH GUN IN ACTION.

To face page 82.

we were beautifully straddled by a salvo of four 1914.
medium-calibre shells from some unkind fellow
away in the south.   This reception was repeated
four times, hitting my office and my servant, who
was in the act of dressing a chicken for dinner, so
we cleared out to the west for a spell.   At this
time a hostile airman came up and manœuvred
about overhead whilst we were shunting.   When
he had gone we went on again to the Comines
line and opened fire again from K. 33.   Ypres and
Zillebeke were being shelled again, and we could
see stuff falling around our other position which
we had just left.   Three hostile balloons were seen
going up away to the south, and some time afterwards a battery started shelling the station behind
us.   Not liking the trap, we retreated and fled
through the station to wait on the other side of
it till they had finished, informing the Headquarters of this; in reply I was told that the
Hollebeke battery had not fired since our last
firing at it, and was thought to have been forced
to move at last.   The Hun eventually tired of it,
so after seeing all clear through the station, we
ran out again on the Roulers line in time to carry
out the dusk bombarding programme, and then
return for the night.

That evening we received a copy of the following
telegram, sent on to us from Littlejohns at
Boulogne:

From First Lord of the Admiralty.

" Am very glad to hear of good work of the armoured trains. Tell your men."

The Germans had attacked during the day, but we had apparently expected it, for an officer made prisoner the day before had stated that they were going to make a last effort to break through, and that if they failed they were going to give it up and take up defensive positions. The 2nd Corps had borne the major part of the attack between the Menin road and the canal. At first we lost a few trenches, but our troops returned to the counter-attack and retook them. Later in the afternoon the enemy tried again on a small sector held by the 3rd Cavalry Division, but the latter stood their ground and drove them back. Our own casualties had been grave enough, but it was said that those of the enemy's were frightful. In one small section alone a thousand German dead bore witness to our men's fine courage. A lot more French troops were arriving in the area and were to be met everywhere. I learnt that they were going to take over the whole front here from us during the next few days.

Nov. 18th.   In the morning we went off to the Comines line, and the 6-inch opened fire from K. 32½ on to a battery south-west of Zandevoorde, whilst I took the 4·7 section up farther to see if a nearer

position was possible; however, the lines were too 1914.
badly wrecked abreast the Zillebeke Lake, where
there was no cover or straight line, so I had to
return to the 6-inch position, and join in from there.

Towards midday a battery commenced dropping
shells in our area, and some fell too uncomfortably
close, so we shifted position on the Roulers line·
To get there I found we had to run the gauntlet
of some shelling of the south-east corner of Ypres,
and in fact had a narrow escape of being knocked
off the line by a salvo which passed between the
two sections and landed in a pond on the far side
of the railway embankment.   At 2.30 we were in
action again with the 6-inch on the Gheluvelt
targets and the 4·7 on Zandevoorde.   Within a
quarter of an hour we got the same reception as
yesterday, being straddled again, splinters from
the second salvo hitting the 6-inch bogie and its
engine, and wounding the driver.   Farther in rear
a shell landed alongside a wagon loaded with
4.7 cartridges and riddled it, but luckily did no
other damage, though I removed a splinter from
the base of one cartridge where it was embedded
alongside the adapter, having passed through the
box and metal case containing four of the cartridges.
At the same time the station was being shelled, so
in getting clear we had to pass through that,
which we did as fast as possible, regardless of the
steam-cloud we sent up.   The Germans then let

1914. the station have it properly, turning on a battery
of " Jack Johnsons " for over an hour. I had to
report that both lines east of the station were untenable and the station impassable at present.

At 4.30 the shelling ceased and I went forward
to look at our line. It was still intact, but there
was an awful mess all round; I counted forty
huge craters within a space of 100 yards square,
but it was now too late for us to go out again.
A record to the effect that we had been heavily
shelled but were undamaged appeared that evening
in the Corps *Bulletin.*

Nov. 19th.   As we approached the station on our way east
next day a greeting of heavy shells landed in the
station and stopped our progress in that direction;
but not to be balked, I took the 6-inch into the
station between two salvos and shunted on to the
Boesinghe line, where we found a position at K. 55
and opened fire on one of the Zandevoorde targets.
Sleet was falling, turning later to a steady snow-
fall.

Early in the afternoon the shelling ceased, for
the Germans had perhaps stopped for dinner as
usual, so I ran out on the Roulers line with the
4.7 section and opened fire for half an hour to
relieve the 6-inch and then returned. We had
timed the Huns' meal hour nicely, for the shelling
of the station soon began, continuing till dusk.

Things were very much quieter as we passed

MY OFFICE.

To face page 86.

eastward in the morning, though the main square was still receiving the usual marked attention; we went straight into action with all guns on the new positions of two batteries in front of Klein-Zillebeke, returning after half an hour's firing. Whilst coming back through the station a battery opened fire on it, one shell of the first salvo landing under the tail of the last 4·7 bogie, smothering it with mud. From the apparent direction it seemed to be the same fellow as had chased me off the Comines line previously, but this time there was no doubt as to his line, for when the shelling ceased I went forward and found seven holes in my line; six had burst and blown up the rails, but the seventh was a dud, and the base of the shell was clearly visible down the hole in the hard clay. It was a 4·1-inch, and the direction of the hole gave the line of the battery quite easily.

Unable to go east any more, we put the 6-inch into action again from the Boesinghe line, and then went back to Poperinghe after dark.

When I reported my line of direction at Headquarters the General said I was quite right, and that airmen had to-day located a battery hidden in the front edge of the wood, and there sure enough was the line of direction I had laid off. He also told me that now all our troops had been relieved by the French, and that he himself was off in the morning, so that our co-operation

1914. here was at an end.   He made some kind remarks on our work when I said *au revoir*, and later sent the following report to the base:

"The Armoured Train 'Jellicoe,' under the command of Lieutenant R——, joined the 1st Corps on November 15th. The train has been employed daily in connection with the operations east of Ypres in firing upon the batteries, roads, communications, and places of assembly of the enemy. Owing to the enclosed nature of the country, all firing has been conducted by map and compass, and no direct observation has been practicable. It is therefore not possible to state with any certainty what the effect of this fire may have been, but prisoners have admitted that our guns have been a source of loss to them. Lieutenant R—— has displayed great energy and keenness, and he and his crew of the armoured train have done excellent work. They have been under fire daily, and it is due to the skill with which Lieutenant R—— has manœuvred his train that he has escaped without casualty.

"(Signed)   H. T. Horne,
"*Major-General, R.A., 1st Army Corps.*"

The following extract from one of the local dailies is of amusing interest:

"Pour remplir les temps de silence il y a le train blindé qui sévit sous les remparts même de la ville et dont la plus grosse pièce envoie ses

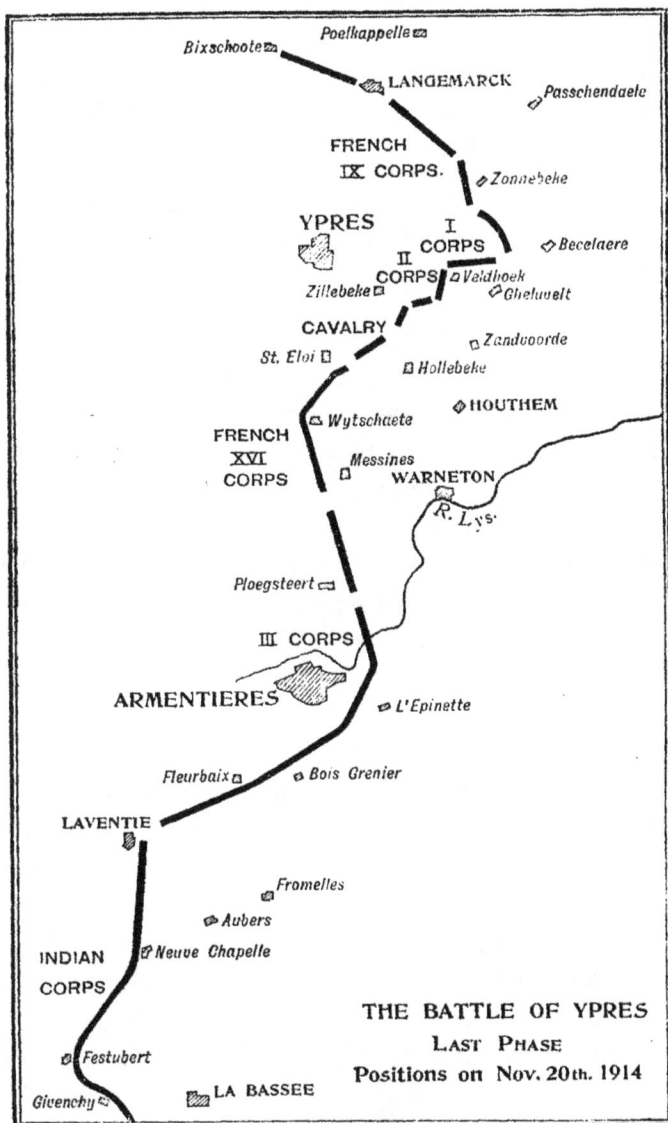

Bixschoote
Poelkappelle
LANGEMARCK
Passchendaele

FRENCH
IX CORPS.
Zonnebeke

YPRES
I CORPS
Becelaere
II CORPS
Veldhoek
Zillebeke
Gheluvelt

CAVALRY
Zandvoorde
St. Eloi
Hollebeke
HOUTHEM
Wytschaete

FRENCH
XVI
CORPS
Messines
WARNETON
R. Lys.

Ploegsteert

III CORPS

ARMENTIERES
L'Epinette

Fleurbaix
Bois Grenier

LAVENTIE

Fromelles
Aubers
Neuve Chapelle
INDIAN
CORPS

THE BATTLE OF YPRES
LAST PHASE
Positions on Nov. 20th. 1914

Festubert
Givenchy
LA BASSEE

1914. projectiles à 20 kilomètres. Cet engin diabolique
est manœuvré par un marin anglais qui fume sa
pipe avec un flegme effroyant. La détonation est
telle que les remparts eux-mêmes en sont ébranles,
et l'air troué par l'obus vibre jusqu'au bout de
l'horizon. ' Little Willy ' c'est le nom du canon,
est un voisin bien incommode, mais il doit faire
de bonne besogne."

During the afternoon I was able to telephone to
Littlejohns at the base, and arranged to go to Dunkerque to get rid of a large number of empties and
to fill up with ammunition. Our guns also were
considerably coppered and required cleaning or
replacing by others. During the afternoon we
arrived there and went on the quays; there I joined
the hospital yacht *Liberty* alongside, and aboard
her enjoyed a hot bath and a most excellent dinner.
Later the Belgian train of 4·7's arrived with
Captain Servais; it was now known as the
" Deguise," so named after our recent Commander-
in-Chief at Antwerp. They had been engaged with
the Belgian army before Dixmude on and off for
the last month.

Six more 4·7 guns arrived from England, so I
had the job of shifting all our guns and sending
the old ones home.

When this was completed I left for Boulogne
and laid up the train for a rest at the station of
Wimereux. Some of the men were sent home on

four days' leave,* and for the first time since 1914.
leaving two months ago, the crew were paid; they
thoroughly enjoyed the chance of spending a few
coins, for the only money on the train had been
the few pounds I had brought out with me.

On December 1st I got leave myself and went
home to England for seven days.

* See Appendix III.

CHAPTER IV

WINTER BEFORE LA BASSÉE

1914. UPON return from leave I found that things were very quiet at the front, and that only one train was being used at a time, Ridler being at Ypres with his repaired 6-inch guns. All our own repairs had been completed, and with the exception of a few men who got leave to go home in turn, we were ready for service when required. Meanwhile to keep fit we started a routine of route marches each forenoon, whilst each afternoon we arranged a football match, followed by a couple of hours' leave in the village. However, plenty of rain and gales interrupted our work and made times rather boring, so that the joy was unanimous when we received orders on December 21st to get ready at once and leave for Bethune that night.

Arriving there the same night, a message greeted us saying that at the moment the 1st Corps were taking over the sector from the Indians, and orders would be issued to us from the former later on. We learnt that the enemy had attacked Givenchy on the 20th and forced our troops back almost to Dec. 22nd. our guns. Our first counter-attack had only suc-

92

ceeded in regaining Givenchy itself, but the 1st 1914. Corps had arrived and to-day were going straight into the fight. That something extra lively was in progress at the front was obvious from the din we could hear as far back as Bethune, and it was quite irritating having to wait to join in. By the end of the day our men had driven all the enemy back to his original lines.

During the afternoon of the following day General Horne, who still commanded the Corps artillery, came on board and told me to meet him next morning at Beuvry. On arriving as arranged, he took me to the Headquarters of the 1st Division, where I met Brigadier-General Fanshawe, C.R.A., under whom I was directed to work.

It was decided that I should begin by co-operating with aircraft, the means of communicating now being by Smith's Morse lamps and a code, and so get a decent calibration of my new guns. That afternoon we went forward and selected a position ready to open fire, but no airman arrived. The nights were very cold now and the dawn showed a heavy frost on the ground—a proper Christmas. white Christmas morning. 1914.

I had a large selection of targets to choose from, and found a very convenient position to the east of the canal junctions. A dense wood lay close by us on the left, behind which we could go for shelter in case of the necessity of a screen, but in front of

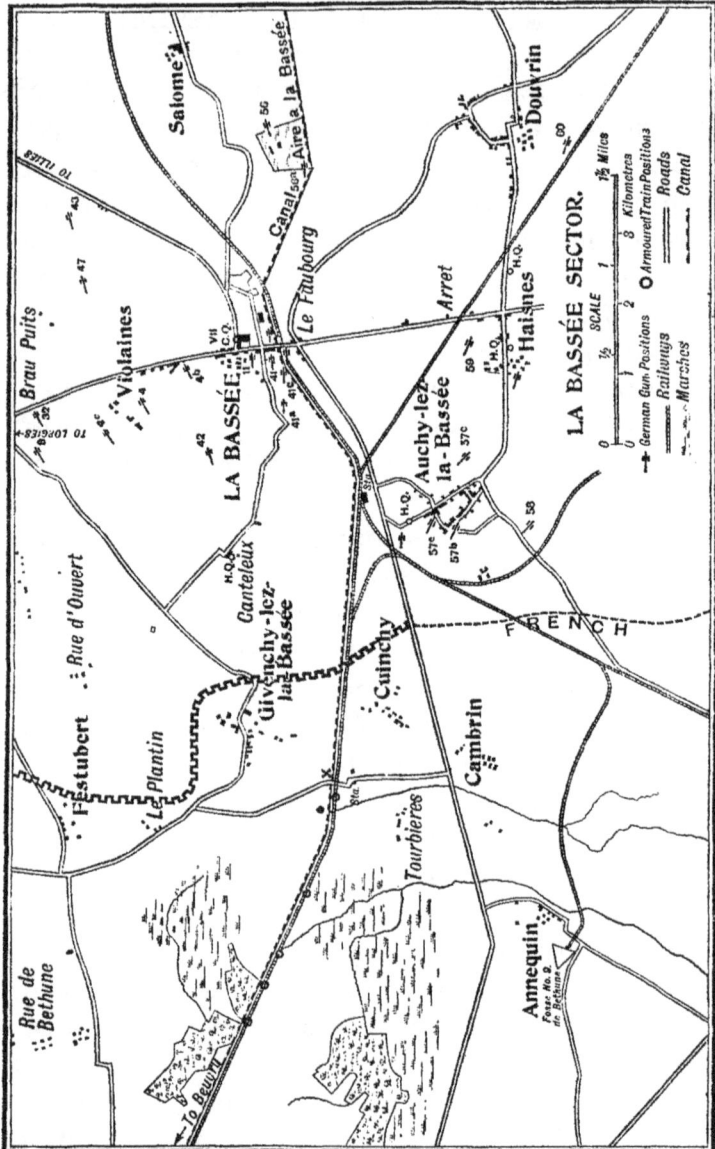

LA BASSÉE SECTOR.

SCALE

Kilometres

German Gun Positions
Armoured Train Positions
Railways
Roads
Marches
Canal

Salomé

Aire à la Bassée

Canal

Douvrin

TO LILLE

Brau Puits

Violaines

Le Faubourg

Arret

Haisnes

TO LORGIES

LA BASSÉE

Auchy-lez-
la-Bassée

Canteleux

Givenchy-lez-
la-Bassée

Cuinchy

Festubert

Rue d'Ouvert

Le Plantin

Cambrin

FRENCH

Rue de
Bethune

Tourbières

Annequin

To Beuvry

this it was possible for anyone on the La Bassée 1914. Church to spot our gun-flashes. A field battery was posted in emplacement on each of our quarters, the 113th and 118th. No particular firing orders were given me for the day, perhaps because it was Christmas, but my first list of targets included a wood and château at Coisne, which was said to be the cover of a bivouac and supply columns, and this seemed to be a nice spot upon which to leave our Christmas card. At a quarter past noon I ran the train out and fired five salvos of high-explosive into the area and then returned to our dinner.

We had our Christmas mail of parcels, but by some unfortunate accident the Royal presents which were served out to every man in France missed us. This was the fault at the base, but we got them some three months later.

On returning to Beuvry, I found that the Headquarters had moved to a more permanent billet in Bethune, where I enjoyed an excellent dinner with the Divisional Commander, General Hashing, and his staff. My midday present to the enemy had amused them, and indeed it seemed curious compared with the rumours we heard of peace, picnics, and a football match with the Saxons just north of us. Opinion on this item varied.

Beuvry Station became our Headquarters each night, but I had to run back to Bethune on an engine to report as usual.

1914.   After a hard frost during the night the day was brilliantly clear; we waited behind the cover of the woods for our observer to arrive.   The method Dec. 26th. of co-operating employed was that the aeroplane would fly towards the target, and when he could see it clearly, the round would be fired as he turned to one side to watch for the burst.   When he had seen it, he returned and signalled the result by lamp.   The aeroplane was generally kept to one side of the line of fire and in no particular constant position relatively to the guns, so as not to become too obvious an indication of their position and range.

In these early days of the war wireless had not reached the state of perfection required for spotting and signalling which it did later on.   Our airman appeared overhead about 11 a.m. and we opened fire, but after several trial shots I had to give it up, for he could not see the bursts, which were hidden in the woods.   Later when he tried again on another target he said it had come over too misty to spot, so we had to give it up for the day.

We tried again next day, the airman saying he could see No. 41 clearly enough for spotting, but when we got going the mist was very hindering; however, we were eventually able to start, and were soon put on the mark.   It is very difficult to judge what allowances to make for the cordite

H.Q. STAFF AND THE CREW.

To face page 96.

when it is open to all changes of temperature; a 1914. 10 per cent. drop in range was often experienced.

Each evening whilst at Bethune I was able to purchase a copy of *The Times* of the preceding day for the sum of thirty centimes; this was a great blessing.

For the next two days we had a strong gale, and the rain came down in torrents, so aeroplane work was quite impossible, and artillery at a standstill. The only shelling of any note was the evening's plastering of Annequin slag-heaps and a few stray shots into Givenchy.

Half along the line towards Pont Fixe and a couple of hundred yards in front of our firing position there were two high standards which in times of peace were used for carrying the cables of the canal electric system. On the top of one of these I rigged a block, so that I could be hauled up in a boatswain's chair. So long as I kept on the rear side of the trellis-work structure, it was possible that I should not be seen by the enemy's observers. From that height I could just make out the general lines of the trench system, except when the rise of Givenchy shut out the view; also I got a particularly good view of most of the railway triangle in front of Cuinchy. La Bassée was in full view, and with glasses I could descry figures moving about in the tower of La Bassée Church; they were no doubt German observers,

1914. and I itched to have a shot at them, but so long as the Germans did not shell Bethune it was understood that we would not shell La Bassée, where there were still large numbers of civilians.

That evening an amusing contribution was included in the daily *Bulletin* under the heading of—

VERSES BY A SUBALTERN.

A is our Army, which with impunity
      Bill said he'd smash at his first opportunity.
B is for Babe, who is called St. Nazaire,
      No longer the home of the gallant and fair.
C is the Charge of the Scottish of London;
      From the papers you'd argue they only had done one.
D is De Wet, who thought it was wiser
      To break his allegiance and follow the Kaiser.
E is the End of this horrible war;
      It will probably last for a century more.
F are the Flares which never seem lacking,
      Sent up by the Germans to see who's attacking.
G are the Germans, a race much maligned:
      A more peace-loving people you hardly can find.
H are the Huns, their nearest of kin;
      A pastoral people they are said to have been.
I am the writer, a perfect nonentity—
      That is the reason I hide my identity.
J is the Joy on the faces of men
      When they're told they must go down for rations at ten.
K is the Kaiser, who's said to be balmy;
      We always feel safe when he's leading his army.
L is the Lake that protects us from fire;
      They call it a trench when the weather is drier.
M stands for mud, to describe which foul stuff
      Violent blasphemy's hardly enough.
N is the Noise which we generally hear
      On the night when the Germans are issued with beer.

1914.

O is the Order, obeyed with a yawn,
   Of " Stand to your arms !—it's an hour till dawn."
P is the Post, which generally brings
   Parcels of perfectly valueless things.
Q is the Question we all do abhor,
   Concerning the probable end of the war.
R stands for Rum, and also the Russians—
   Our two greatest allies when fighting the Prussians.
S, as you know, always stands for Supplies,
   Whose excellent qualities no one denies.
T is Tobacco, that beautiful stuff;
   And, thanks be to Heaven, we've now got enough
U stands for Uhlan, who's gained notoriety
   Both through his kindness and wonderful piety.
V is the Voice of the turtle, which bird
   Has been turned into stew, so it's no longer heard.
W stands for Wine, Women, and War;
   We'll see to the first when the latter is o'er.
X is a perfectly horrible letter;
   I'll leave it alone, and I couldn't do better.
Y stands for Ypres, which the Germans desire;
   They shelled it as soon as they had to retire.
Z stands for Zeppelins, who long wished to raid
   A Circus, a Square, and a certain Arcade.

Our airman did not arrive overhead till noon
next day, when we started ranging on No. 41, but Dec. 30th.
he did not stay long, and went down home after
several signals of " Unobserved." He ran out to
see us and saw that some other battery was firing
at the same time as ourselves, so that he could not
pick out our bursts, which were short; the cordite
must have still been frozen, though the weather
was now milder. Whilst we had been firing a
German sausage went up in the direction of Lorgies
and as he must have seen us, we might expect

1914. something over us soon, so retired a bit to wait. However, nothing arrived in our area. Late in the afternoon we ran out to behind Cuinchy Station, bombarded the cross-roads at Illies for twenty minutes, and then returned home. That evening I had a bath and dined at the Headquarters, a pleasure which became a weekly occurrence each Thursday.

By now arrangements were in operation so that the troops coming out of the trenches were taken to the baths at Bethune, their uniform thoroughly cleaned, and their underclothing changed; my own sailors went through this once a fortnight. This excellent service must have improved the general health of everyone considerably, besides checking the objectionable little friends that used to visit so many of the men.

Dec. 31st.   After we had gone out next morning a Chaplain visited us and held a Communion Service. I went forward to our reserve trenches to look into the possibility of making a forward observation post for us; but the brewery at Pont Fixe seemed the best, for though being some short distance in rear, it afforded an excellent view of the terrain. Towards 4 p.m. a violent shelling broke out in front of us and around Givenchy and Pont Fixe. No special orders arrived, so we opened fire on the Coisne area. The firing died down in front, so we went home, where I learnt that the Germans had

attacked and occupied an advanced machine-gun 1915.
post of ours.

Everyone had been very careful with their ammunition, as it was very scarce; we were better off than
anyone, for our allowance averaged three times
that of other batteries per gun. At midnight I
struck " sixteen bells " on our ship's bell, for
which a 6-inch cylinder served the purpose.

During the following forenoon orders arrived to Jan. 1st.
bombard the eastern apex of the triangle, and a
note to be prepared to increase the rate of fire if
ordered.   From my position up the standard the
target was in full view, so we started in at once
and continued slowly. Soon afterwards a battery
of small calibre commenced shelling us, but everything passed over my head and fell into the canal
in front of the train. Again during the afternoon
whilst we were firing it came back, but much
closer this time. I began to think that my friends
in the church at La Bassée could see me moving
up and down the standard. After a couple of
shrapnel bursts behind me and one almost alongside my ear, I thought it time to get down. Hardly
had I set foot on the ground before they hit the
top, knocking it clean off, and sending my block
to bits at my feet. First thoughts were best that
time, and I felt very glad that I had not stayed
up there too long to think about it. We learnt
that the German attack yesterday had eventually

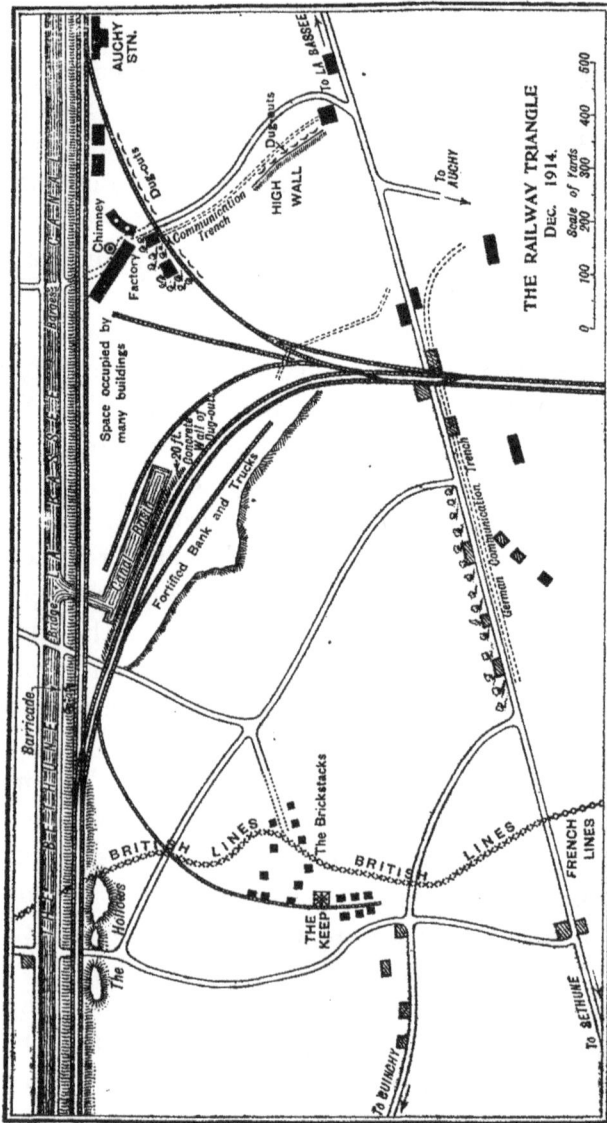

THE RAILWAY TRIANGLE
DEC. 1914.

Scale of Yards
0   100   200   300   400   500

AUCHY STN.

To LA BASSÉE

To AUCHY

Chimney
Factory

Communication Trench
Dug-outs
Dug-outs

HIGH WALL

Space occupied by many buildings

20 ft. Concrete Wall of Dug-outs

Fortified Bank and Trucks

German Communication Trench

Barricade

The Harrows
The

BRITISH LINES

The Brickstacks

THE KEEP

BRITISH LINES

FRENCH LINES

To BÉTHUNE

To BUVIGNY

succeeded in taking a trench of ours. Later a 1915.
general bombardment was ordered for five minutes,
my particular target being the Lorgies cross-road.

The following day was very miserable; raining
and blowing a gale. Movements of troops and the
work of keeping up the supplies for those in the
front line must have been nearly impossible, but
though the A.S.C. people told awful yarns of their
trials, they seemed to get there all right. The
trenches were no more than drains cut through
the country, where existence was an everlasting
punishment—thoughts of which made us realize
how deuced fortunate we were in our warm train.

Our own rations were left each night by the
A.S.C. at the Beuvry Station as they passed
through on their way to the front, and with some
additions from our storeroom our menus continued
to be quite exceptional. The word passed round,
so that my office soon became a stopping-place for
those officers who cared for a yarn and a cup of tea.

Littlejohns came up from Boulogne on a visit, so
that we were able to discuss the need and possibility of getting another officer lent to me to assist
and do the observation work from an advanced O.P.

The next day was much finer, so I set out for
the ruins of what was once a cottage situated near
our trenches, to get a closer view of the interior Jan. 3rd.
of the triangle and the general run of the buildings
there.

1915.   Approaching Givenchy, signs such as " To the Casualty Station," " To Batt. Headquarters," " To Cross Bone Alley," etc., showed the way to the several positions named. The whole village was a maze of trenches, for use when the shelling made the open road too hazardous. Paths wandered in all directions—behind buildings, across gardens, into a house by a door and out again by a hole in the wall, behind heaps of bricks and then under a sunken arch—all selected so as to provide protection from stray bullets and shut out the traffic from the enemy's observers and snipers.

The village was in ruins from end to end—a battered sepulchre. No building was whole; all roofless, hardly a wall without a hole or a huge crack. The shattered remains of the fittings and furniture lying on the floors indicated the class of the former occupants. China crocks and ornaments lay shattered on the shelf. A child's cradle overturned in a corner, vivid pictures in pieces and at all angles on the walls, plaster from the ceiling and bare floor, were the few remaining signs of previous humble occupants; whilst the home of someone more fortunate was evident by the burst upholstering showing springs and padding of a settee, a smashed polished table minus all legs, torn carpets, and smashed bedstead hanging from the shattered beams of the first floor, a tiled hearth and discoloured, splashed wallpaper. Mixed up in

all this dirt lay hundreds of empty tins, bits of 1915.
service kit, sandbags; heaps of straw and old
bedding showed where the soldier had tried to
find rest and shelter.

Moving on, one approached the reserve trenches,
the track to be followed being plainly marked by
sign-posts bearing instructions and directions to
various trenches, etc. If these were not closely
followed a whistle of a bullet would soon force
one to realize that these instructions were put
there for other reasons than directing, as German
snipers were ever on the watch for a chance of
drawing a bead upon the unwary.

Arriving at the ruins, I climbed up very cau-
tiously and carefully looked through a hole in the
wall. From here the objects of the visit were
in full view, whilst in the foreground was a
splendid view of the trenches, the few moving
khaki forms of the sentries, the walls of the
trenches, the piles of sandbags, the shadows of
the dug-outs, and beyond the neutral strip of
grass-covered ground, bordered on both edges by
a jungle of barbed wire.

There on the German parapet lay a few dark
objects—dead Huns shot down at night or tumbled
out over the parapet by their own comrades after
being killed in their trenches, and there left to
rot. The extraordinary silence over the whole
field was occasionally broken by the sharp crack

1915. of a rifle as a sniper tried his luck on some minute object seen to traverse his line of fire laid on the opposite trenches by his observer at the periscope.

On our way back I found a tortoise-shell cat wandering about Cuinchy which looked as if she wanted a home, so I brought her back with me. That afternoon we bombarded a factory in the triangle, spotting from the standard, from which I could locate each burst quite distinctly. A battery replied, but the shells flew wide. Hoping to deceive the other fellow that he had got our line and range, I ceased fire for a spell; he then started firing high-explosive shells for some minutes. When he stopped I continued again. At any rate, if we went on like that it might induce him to expend shell in ploughing up the field on our left, thinking he was keeping us quiet, whereas it was the limit of the day's expenditure that kept us so.

A thick mist hung over the country all next day and no action was taken. Our General visited us and showed me some more targets and areas which required attention.

The Germans found amusement in bombarding a bit of waste land in front of the wood on the left of our position with 8·2-inch guns. The high-explosive they used made huge craters in the wet mud; those had detonated, but the majority only exploded with a loud squelch. I retrieved a fuse intact, which was the type used by the Belgians

and made in a Belgian factory. That night our 1915·
sentry fired on a light which was flickering along
the telephone wires and did not reply to challenges.
Later again in the early morning someone was seen
hovering round our guns; the challenge got no
reply, so the sentry opened fire, upon which some
of the other men jumped out and joined in. However, no trace could be found of any visitor, but
rumours of spies were quite common; and orders
had been made that no single person was to
approach any battery at night, and fire was to be
opened at once on any loitering figures.

We heard that Ridler had returned to England,
and that another officer, M. Gould, had come out
to take over his train.

The following morning was again misty, but Jan. 5th.
clearing later in the day, we were able to carry out
a bombardment for half an hour on the far corner
of the triangle. During the day one of the 6-inch
guns arrived to reinforce my train. I now kept
the 6-inch on one set of metals and the 4·7 section
on the other. Whilst shunting in Beuvry during
the evening my wagon was derailed, but with the
assistance of a wreckage gang from Bethune we
got it replaced by midnight.

Light rain began falling during the following
day, although we had had a frosty night. During
the forenoon I calibrated the 6-inch on a target in
the triangle, relieving it by the 4·7's later. In the

1915. afternoon I tried the effect of the 6-inch on some railway-trucks which were still on the railway forming the south-western face of the triangle.   It was said that these trucks had been lately turned into machine-gun shelters, whilst the high embankment itself beneath, which had a concrete face on the far side, was a warren of dug-outs. We got a couple of direct hits on the trucks, lifted one up on to another, and the bursting of the common shell against their sides was quite picturesque.   The 4·7 section shelled some barges lying in the basin which were used also as shelters for troops.

At Beuvry that evening the Chaplain boarded us and held a service.   During the night my cat wandered off, but was brought in at dawn by my Belgian railway guard.

Another period of gales and rain intervened, and then we commenced the programme of systematically ranging all the various batteries of the Corps upon portions of the triangle; those of our own Division (the 1st) were allotted the forenoon— each battery having a certain period of time in which to register—finishing up with all batteries doing a combined bombardment for a few minutes. This triangle was rapidly becoming a most important area; it afforded very good shelter for the assembly of troops, and compared with the surrounding country was a very excellent jumping-off

ground for an attack.   However, we were going 1915.
to make it as untenable as possible for whichever
battalion was there as a garrison.

Our period was from 10 a.m., when we commenced registering each gun upon the line of
trucks we had previously shelled.   From my
spotting position up the standard I could get a
good view, and once again one of the 6-inch shell
disarranged a truck; at 12.45 we all fired together,
the result being a fury of shell-bursts and explosions which must have made things very un-
comfortable for the Hun.

Later we learnt that our first round from the
6-inch which had ranged short had landed in a
German trench, causing its garrison to bolt, and
in turn became the target for our troops' rifles.

Naturally all this did not go on without drawing
a reply, but in the area around us the shell continued to fall harmlessly into the neighbouring
field.   A few large shells were thrown around the
Beuvry Station during the day, and one landed in
the courtyard of the Gorre Château, where it burst,
killing fifteen Indians and wounding forty-two
others.

The bombarding continued next day, our
period commencing at 10.30 a.m., when the 6-inch
continued as before, but we were ranged along the Jan. 9th.
northern embankment facing the canal and on the
barge ferry there.   Field guns started placing

1915. unpleasant shell round my standard, so I had to come down; one lesson had been enough. More to the rear I tried a railway signal-post, from which a good view of the triangle was possible.

Near by was a small house used by some old women, who still lived there in spite of their close proximity to the shells. Now that I had to come back near them, they asked what I thought about their safety in future, as things were daily growing warmer; and though I did not expect them to follow the advice, they eventually did so in the course of a day or so. What wonderful women these were, up till now tilling their small patch of soil daily, paying little heed to the bursting of shells around them, and so hardened that the sight of aircraft flying overhead did not even inspire sufficient curiosity to cause them to look at them. And yet the houses in the east and their church on the skyline, which for all their lives had been within their view, were no longer, as they lay in tumbled heaps of bricks, stones, and mortar. A couple of white crosses in their garden mark the graves of two Englishmen who had fallen in their defence, as they had for their own kin. They were ever dressed in black, and knew too well that those noïses and explosions always in their ears plainly told of more graves and more women that would wear black.

It is little wonder if few smiles are to be seen

on the faces of such women. They have seen and 1915.
heard the red anger of war, not in illustrated
papers nor cinema shows, but at first hand, with
their own eyes and ears—in the white clouds of
shrapnel and black volcanoes of high explosives, in
the flames of burning houses, in the thunder of the
guns and the shrieking of shells, in the groans of the
wounded and the shattered forms of the dead.

All the country-side is full of such women, of
whom one could say she has a husband, a son, or
a lover out there in front, as every male relative
and friend, old and young, wearing the blue
uniform of France, is serving his country either in
the battle or in the workshop.

During the whole remaining period of our stay
on this sector and the many lively days to come,
these women returned each day to carry on their
work on the land, walking miles to and fro. Shells
would plough huge holes •in their field, but they
were filled in during the day and the neatness of
their plots restored.

At 1.23 p.m. the combined shoot took place with
picturesque effect, bringing down a heavy shelling
upon Givenchy, whilst large shells ploughed through
the wood on our left, and a field gun got quite close
to us. I was covered with mud from one burst,
and another landed alongside my wagon, though
far behind; still, we saw it out.

The German troops before us at this time con-

1915. sisted of battalions of the 7th and 14th Corps, of which the 56th, 57th, and 116th Regiments of the 14th Division were just north of the canal, and the 169th and 170th Regiments of the 29th Division were at the triangle.

The following account of a ruse used with some success to deceive the enemy (so someone had dreamt) was received from our 4th Division, and promulgated for general information under the heading of:

TRICKS FOR DECEIVING THE ENEMY.

A dashing experiment has lately been carried out by Lt. Smythe-Buggins, of the 2nd Artists, which if tried again, with improvements suggested below, can hardly fail to be of great tactical value. Lt. S.-B. is in close touch with the theatrical costumiers and stage-property trade, and indeed appeared once as an understudy in the Drury Lane pantomime, taking up at short notice the part of the Rajah of Bhong's camel's hind-legs (and tail). He obtained at his own expense a property cow (invoice, Appendix A), fitted with bullet-proof loins. This cow was carried by a specially selected party of men to a position about half-way between the lines of barbed wire, opposite a German battalion reported to be recruited from a district entirely agricultural. The line of trenches at the selected point ran due north and south. The cow was placed in a grazing position, head to the west. Before dawn, Lt. S.-B. took up his position in the belly of the cow, taking with him stores detailed in Appendix B.

At 6.30 a.m. Lt. S.-B. brought an imitation 1915. thrush into action. By this it was hoped to induce a bucolic atmosphere of unwariness in the enemy. This part of the experiment was a failure. The first intimation of the enemy's interest in the cow was at 9.45 a.m. (by which time the imitation thrush had run down and refused to function).

Shortly before this Lt. S.-B. had sounded two blasts on the motor-horn. It was then that he became aware of a determined hostile attempt to milk the cow, evidently made by a German who had crawled in from one flank, and was therefore not visible from the spyhole. Realizing his mistake, the German uttered a loud exclamation of disgust, and was promptly shot from our trenches in rear. The enemy's trenches then replied to our fire, giving Lt. S.-B. a series of very good targets from his commanding position. Of these he made the fullest use. His position, however, was made particularly hazardous by the fact (elicited from the wounded German afterwards) that the enemy in front of him had had no meat for several days. Determined efforts were made for several hours by the enemy to shoot the cow, with the evident intention of recovering the carcase for consumption later.

Finding that their efforts were unsuccessful, a machine gun was brought to bear, and after the expenditure of a large quantity of ammunition, the cow was eventually overthrown. During this bombardment Lt. S.-B.'s conduct was beyond all praise, and he kept up a rapid fire to his front until his ammunition was exhausted. But on the overthrow of the cow he was forced to take refuge in

8

1915. a very cramped position in the armoured portion. A spirited contest now ensued for the recovery of the body between the Germans and the Artists. Grapnels were flung freely on both sides. Our casualties in this phase of the incident were I regret to say, heavy (Appendix C) and mainly self-inflicted.

Our Battalion, however, was fortunate in having the service of Lance-Corporal Murphy (who starred in the provinces as the champion Harpoonist and Boomerang Thrower). This N.C.O. succeeded in engaging the cow's horns at the seventh effort, and the body was successfully hauled into our advanced trench. Lt. S.-B. was withdrawn at dusk in an exhausted condition.

The ruse, though not entirely successful, owing to the miscalculation as to the psychological effect on the enemy, was nevertheless of practical value. Not only was considerable damage inflicted by Lt. S.-B.'s fire, but it is believed that the enemy's moral in this section has been considerably lowered as a result of their disappointment in the matter of a supply of fresh meat.

For a future occasion it is suggested:

(1) That a bullock, not a cow, be provided. This will overcome any likelihood of premature discovery, as was threatened by the milking incident.

(2) That the bullock be a dead bullock, be entirely plated, and placed moribund.

(3) That to prevent any enterprising enemy from coming too close, and to add to the illusion, the stores detailed in Appendix D to be supplied.

In conclusion, I strongly recommend that the 1915.
conduct of Lt. S.-B., who has added gallantry to
ingenuity, be suitably recognized.

(Signed)   L. TICK-BEERBOHM,
   *Colonel Commanding 2nd Artists (Gaby's
   Own) Rifles.*

APPENDIX A.

Invoice.

	£
To property cow with movable ears, jointed tail, pliable udders complete, hams lined ⅜ inch steel, spyhole in orifice, orifice No. 2 enlarged for rifle, painted 3 coats in black and white	41
Packing-case if not returned	1
Freight	4
	46

APPENDIX B.

Stores.

Thrushes, imitation, pottery, with marble	1	in No.
Horns, motor, bass note	1	,,
Rations, iron	1	,,
Ammunition, rounds..	250	

APPENDIX C.

Flesh wounds, incisions	6	cases
Fractures ..	4	,,
Concussion	10	,,
Contusions	24	,,
Abrasions ..	19	,,

Appendix D.

1915. Sulphuretted hydrogen, tubes 3-inch   ..   3 in No.
     Carbon bisulphate, tubes 3-inch   ..   3   ,,

On the next day we had our programme, promising much interest.

The guns of the whole Corps were to check their registrations until 1.50 p.m., when a ten minutes' combined bombardment was to precede an attack by the 2nd Infantry Brigade upon the lost machine-gun post.

Our period began at 10 a.m., when the 6-inch opened upon the trucks till our aeroplane observer arrived overhead, then we shifted target to the bridge over the canal. The second round, which was too far to the right and thus into the triangle, hit some sort of magazine, putting up a large burst and flame. We at last got the line and straddled, scoring two hits. At 11 a.m. all guns of the Division opened fire for five minutes, after which the 2nd Division on our left carried on with their programme.

Shells from hostile batteries fell in various places, but the nearest to us were in the canal in front of us. Soon afterwards our observer came over to spot the 4·7's on to No. 41, but he went back after a few rounds, having met with some difficulty.

When the Corps bombardment commenced I put

the 6-inch on to the trucks and the 4·7's on to the 1915. eastern apex and barge bridge, and for ten minutes there was an awful din; after which gun-fire was slower and less rowdy, for we all shifted on to hostile battery positions to keep their fire down whilst our men went forward. The rattle of rifle-fire continued for some time, but slowly died away.

The Germans sent up three sausages, at which I fired, but was unable to reach. We continued the slow fire till 3 p.m., when the airman arrived over again, our fire shifting on to No. 41. I got " O.K." signals several times, which meant stradd-ling and line correct, so continued on this target after he had left.

Before night we had achieved quite a good day's work with three successful shoots to our credit.

Good-fortune had followed our attack in the afternoon, for not only had we taken the post, but also an observation post in the Hollows, though it was thought that we would not be able to hold on to the latter position, which was too far ad-vanced and so isolated.

A prisoner taken at the time said that the bombardment yesterday had killed 200 of the triangle's garrison.

That night we lost the advanced post, but firmly held our real objective.

The same artillery routine was carried out next day against the triangle, and as well as that firing Jan. 11th.

1915.

we again opened fire on the bridge, when the aeroplane arrived and got some more hits. At noon the combined bombardment continued for five minutes. That evening Headquarters told me that No. 41 had vacated his former emplacements and was now 500 yards more to the south-west, in position No. 41*a*.

Jan. 12th.

Scattered hostile shelling had already commenced by the time we arrived out next morning, and " whizz-bangs " were bursting over the field on our right. I was greeted by a few shrapnel which fortunately burst wide on one side, but I came back a bit. Before this small stuff stopped they had hit the line, scattering a pile of loose metal and smashing one rail. After midday the shelling increased, and it looked as if something unusual was in progress, so we ran out and opened fire on the Coisne Château, target 41*a*, and the far apex of the triangle. Shells continued to fall around us, but the only damage was from a few splinters striking the 6-inch bogie, and one man being slightly wounded with a cut in the neck from a piece which also carried away his cap in passing. By 3 p.m. the firing had died down, so we ceased also. We heard that the shelling had been the covering to a minenwerfer attack on the post taken by us on the 10th, forcing our garrison out and leaving it once more in the Germans' hands. Towards dusk we gave the Château

grounds another bombardment and then returned. 1915.
That evening a suggestion to relieve us by another
train was made from the base, but eventually
dropped after Headquarters reported on the idea
as undesirable.

Two days' heavy rains followed, making things
impossible for most; even our troops in front of
Festubert had to come out of their trenches to
drier ground in the buildings behind them.   However, towards the close of the second day we were
able to run out and bombard the Château, No. 41a,
and Illies for an hour.

An 8·2-inch howitzer battery had now been Jan. 15th.
located on the western edge of the Château woods,
so we were directed to shell it upon arrival out
next forenoon, during which process we got it
back fairly hot, though as usual the direction was
wrong, and all we received was a bath of mud
and water all over the 6-inch gun, one shell falling
alongside it.   Whilst the crew were going through
the baths in Bethune that evening, Admiral Tufnell,
who was working with the Red Cross here, came
on board to visit our curious ship.

A long spell of miserable weather followed,
during which very little work was done by anyone.
The 8·2 howitzer continued each day to try and
smash up our lines, but nearly always missed—
dropping into the wood on the left, the front edge
of which was gradually moving to the west, as its

1915. trees were blown up or cut off short by the incessant shelling. It was seen that No. 41 had again moved his position, and was now in two sections in emplacements labelled 41c and 42d. We managed to get in an hour's firing one day, when we levelled a series of buildings inside the triangle. Snow fell very heavily one night, affording some amusement, including an unsuccessful attack with snowballs upon the train by the Headquarters units of the 3rd Infantry Brigade.

The following verses were composed by one of our local poets, referring to the shooting of one of our 9·2-inch howitzers which had lately arrived out from home. This addition to our artillery strength was much appreciated, and the pieces were referred to by the infantry by the affectionate term of "Mother." A Boche is supposed to be speaking.

> We've had a slight misfortune with a train,
> And I think we've every reason to complain.
>   It was full of gallant Prussians
>   Going to fight the nasty Russians,
> When overhead they saw an aeroplane.
>   Boom ! Mother !
>   We've picked up several bits
>   Of the late lamented Fritz,
> But we never saw the blooming train again.

> It's really very sad about the town.
> Here lived the Heir-apparent to the crown;
>   It was far from all the stenches
>   Which arise from dirty trenches,
> And we thought the British aeroplanes were done.

BIG AND LITTLE WILLIE

To face page 120.

Boom ! Mother !   1915.
We found the Kronprinz' braces,
But we can't find any traces
Of that Donner Wetter Blitzen Flemish town.

We were loading up our celebrated gun,
After firing Black Marias one by one,
For after careful searches
We had found out two more churches,
When an aeroplane showed black against the sun.
Boom ! Mother !
And although the Kapten pines
Still we can't find any signs
Of our celebrated " Black Maria " gun.

It was not till Wednesday the 20th that we ^{Jan. 20th.} were able to get to work again. For almost two hours that forenoon we fired slowly at several of the targets round La Bassée, and once again we were told that 41 had shifted; this time he was south of the canal by La Faubourg. During the afternoon we opened fire on this position, each calibre in turn, for a couple of hours. This continual shifting of position showed that he did not like it at all, but it was rough luck that the weather was so bad that we could not get some aeroplane spottings and perhaps give more effective punishment.

That evening I had dinner with the 26th Artillery Brigade, and for the first time for many a long day played auction.

The following day brought us a variation, for we had two shoots at a battery at Auchy, No. 57a,

1915. the forward observer of the 113th Field Battery spotting for us and passing his observations back through his battery to which I had run a wire. We got well on to our target both times; the Corps *Bulletin* that night stated that the battery had been silenced. That evening I had dinner with the Headquarters of the 3rd Infantry Brigade, General Butler.

The morning was misty after the night's frost, and our programme with the airman fell through owing to his having to go home at once with Jan.22nd. engine trouble. A newer 6-inch gun arrived during the day to replace the old one, out of which we had already sent 3,000 rounds.

For the first time for a long while we had a German aeroplane over us, and must have been seen, for shortly afterwards the 8·2-inch started again. Luckily they were a bit short and only one shell got the line, but that was enough to make a crater 30 feet in diameter and quite destroyed the left set of metals. During this a most unfortunate affair occurred, for a company of South Wales Borderers came along on their way to the front. Seeing the shelling in front, the officer asked me what I thought about it, and I told him that if he passed over to the south and went up to Tourbierres, he should be safe. Unfortunately, on his way there the shelling checked, and probably thinking it was finished, the soldiers returned to the lines, only to receive the next two 1915. shells, which blew three of them to bits and wounded several more; the latter I sent back to Bethune on an engine.

These large shells have merely a local effect, for they plough into the ground and their burst is confined to a thin cone, all the energy of the explosion passing vertically upwards. Lately an officer belonging to one of our howitzer batteries in front of us stood unharmed whilst two of these shells burst, each 5 yards on either side of him. On the other hand, another officer was hit direct by one of the shell; not a square millimetre of flesh or clothing could be discovered anywhere in the vicinity after a three days' search.

A few days ago during the heavy fighting in progress just south of us, the French got an opportunity of wreaking their revenge for a punishment the Germans had dealt them in a similar manner at Messines in 1914. The French got wind of an attack to be made on them, and which had to cross an open space on the west slope of the ridge. They silently brought up 6 batteries of 75's, and waited until three battalions of the enemy had topped the ridge and then opened fire. It is declared that not one escaped the frightful carnage which followed.

During the following forenoon the Germans sent Jan. 23rd. up a sausage from somewhere beyond Salome,

1915. quite out of reach of any of our artillery.   Determined to have a bang at him, this time I ran out
with the 6-inch to Pont Fixe and opened fire with
shrapnel; he was pulled down at once and taken
away.   However, our advance to almost within
1,000 yards of the Hun had not been unnoticed by
them, and they tried to give us a warm reception for
our audacity, but the shells hit the roofs and
houses around us instead; we did not delay when
we saw the balloon off, but opened out the throttles
and bolted, getting away without a scratch.   The
incident appeared in the evening report, but by
far the most amusing result was a yarn in one of
our home papers some days later.   It ran as
follows:

" One incident of interest has occurred in this
quarter.   A diversion was created by sending one
of our English armoured trains from Bethune to
La Bassée.   It steamed at a great speed along the
line, and for fully three hours the roar of guns
indicated that a furious duel was in progress.   It
was feared that the train had been put out of
action, but towards evening it returned, its armour
absolutely undamaged.   Its gunners and Commander were walking by its side, driving nearly
200 prisoners before them.   Among these were
two hunchbacks and a dwarf. , In passing, I must
mention the almost incredible good-fortune of our
armoured trains.   They have inflicted appalling
damage on the Germans, and all are unscathed,

SNOWBALLING.

A " BLACK MARIA " HOLE.

To face page 124.

their only casualty being one man slightly wounded. 1915. The armoured trains, or our land cruisers as they are called in the ranks, have annihilated whole companies of the enemy. They have fired even their biggest guns during the week. This gives the gunners a weird sensation, for the wheels of the trains jump the rails, but are so made as to regain their position."

Of course the man who wrote that had some brain; though in one point he is correct, for we had fired the 6-inch broadside on, causing the wheels to rise slightly from the rails, but the bogie soon fell back again, for with its armour and a large number of rails suspended over the axles it is a very heavy mass to lift.

Early in the afternoon we registered upon some works in the western apex of the triangle upon which the enemy were expending much energy, the 113th F.B. observer again assisting by spotting us on. After hitting a few times we checked fire, repeating the process at intervals for the rest of the day.

Black Marias started searching us out again, but only damaged the signal-house near the line and a farm on our right; however, in the latter case some of our troops were hit, for when the shelling started they ran out of the farm to see what was happening, and got the next salvo in their midst.

1915.   Later during the day Lieutenant Luard of the
R.G.A. joined me to act as my observer from a
forward O.P., a form of assistance for which we
had long been waiting.   We went forward in the
Jan. 24th. morning and selected a position among the twisted
beams and rafters of the Pont Fixe Brewery from
which he could get a clear view, and ran out the
telephone cables.   At this time the Germans had
turned their 8·2's on to the Givenchy locks of the
canal, so we opened fire upon the position No. 56.
This shelling of the locks continued all day, 125
shells falling all around it—11 tons of metal—
but luckily not damaging it enough to break it.
It was soon realized that their aim was to smash
the locks and flood the country behind our lines,
for the water-level on their side was higher; and
we afterwards learnt that they had formed a big
head of water with which to complete the job.
Any future attempt was stalled off by filling the
lock itself with thousands of bags of sand, and
sinking a barge full of sand, in bags, across the
width of the canal.

During the afternoon we opened fire once more
on the bridge over the canal by the triangle, Luard
spotting from the new O.P.   The bridge had been
hit by us often before, but in spite of all twisted
beams, etc., the Germans were able to run wooden
planks across it and make a good enough passage.
The only way out of it was to try and destroy one

of the brick supports on one bank; then it would 1915. all fall into the canal.

Soon after our arrival out the following morning the enemy opened up a violent shelling, especially Jan. 25th the area all round and in front of Givenchy. Realizing something was up, I was in the act of moving the train forward to retaliate, when down came a salvo on top of the train, killing one engine-driver and wounding several of the crew. One of them, a driver of the other gun engine, was hit in seven places about his body, and his clothes were torn off him in ribbons. With his aid we got the guns back 200 yards, but before we were ready to go again large numbers of troops were assembling near us, so that we could not fire, for it would only draw down a fire upon them. It was said that the Germans had attacked and taken some of our positions, and that a counter-attack was preparing.

It was not till 9.45 that our area was cleared of the majority of the troops and at this time our orders, of particular interest to us, arrived and read:

To Armoured Train.

" 1st Corps have ordered La Bassée to be shelled. Will you please carry this out.':

It appeared that the Germans had fired some shells into Bethune from a long-range gun, and

1915. we were to take our revenge in this way. I ran out and put all guns on to this target, picking out the position of the Headquarters of the 7th Corps, which were just beyond the church. We also fired at other good targets, such as the main bridge over the canal and the station in La Bassée.

Black Marias started coming over again, so that we had to drop back a hundred yards and recommence. During this a battalion of the Gloucesters were passing on the left of the canal, and unhappily got a couple of shells, which cost them several casualties, including an officer and three men killed.

Towards noon the details of the position in front and the orders for the counter-attack reached us, the latter being timed for 1 p.m., my particular target being the canal embankment of the triangle to hold reinforcements from that direction.

The Germans had mined and blown up the trench occupied by the Scots Guards, had captured it and others to the south, so that our line had fallen back into a straight line in front of Givenchy. A secondary attack in front of Givenchy had caused a small set-back, and the French on the south side of the La Bassée road had been driven back to our alignment. However, we still held the " Keep "—a brick fortress in the midst of the brick-fields, wherein our men were surrounded but holding out.

When the bombardment started we kept the 1915.
4·7 section in action against the reinforcement and
the 6-inch upon the 7th Corps Headquarters,
where already two fires were raging as a result of
our previous firing. By 2.30 p.m. the firing sub-
sided, so we reduced our rate, occasionally firing
a few rounds along the embankment.

Our counter-attack had completely driven the
enemy from our lines at Givenchy, having been
repulsed five times with heavy loss; whilst before
Cuinchy we had cleared most of the brick-stacks,
and with a small exception had regained our own
lines again. Altogether it was considered that the
Hun had come off second-best, for his losses were
considerably higher than ours, and though he still
held a small bit of our ground, he had not been
able to withstand our counter-attack in the main
part. The prisoners which filed past our position
were a motley crowd, very much shattered and
extremely glad at being our side of the lines.

At 4 p.m. the battery at Auchy was reported as
being in action, so I turned our 4·7's on to it,
quickly silencing the enemy, as was also reported
from the 113th F.B. observer.

The following is an extract from a letter written
by a German killed to-day. He writes:

" In La Bassée something special will happen in
a few days. You will read of it in the papers,

9

1915. then the dust will fly. I have had luck here, and have several times looked death in the face. But bad weeds don't fade. Peace must not be thought of. This must surely go beyond March.

> " Always lacking, never slacking,
> Never for a bullet asking,

and when I come back I will tell you about Anno '14-'15, and bring you a fine souvenir. Otherwise I am in good health.

> Our hair has grown like manes,
> And soap, it is a stranger,
> We never clean our teeth
> And shirts are never changed.
>
> Our clothes are always soaked,
> Our bellies often empty.
> Of beer and wine, alas !
> No drop remains to tempt me.
>
> Our shoes and socks are bogged
> Of mud you've heard some rumour;
> One thing that still keeps dry,
> And that's our sense of humour."

I was now left with only the 6-inch gun and one 4·7, the other two having been recalled to Boulogne. We made a determined attempt against the bridge during the forenoon, and got four direct hits out of twenty rounds, but the enemy had piled a heap of earth against the buttress, which had to be blown away first, so that little real damage was done. A revised list of targets received that night gave us the positions of four regimental headquarters requiring attention, and

also the news that 41 had once again moved south 1915.
of La Bassée to 41e.

Next morning was very cold and snow was
falling.   I was directed to try and bring down a
tall chimney in the triangle which was supposed
to be an enemy observation post.   For a long time
the enemy had been endeavouring to do the same
to the Brewery smoke-stack, but though it now
resembled a cullender, it had withstood every
bombardment, as also our O.P. in rear of it.

It was by no means an easy matter to hit such
a thin unseen target at 5,000 yards, but I used a
landmark for laying and put lateral corrections
on the deflection scale.   After twenty rounds,
during which we obtained three direct hits, one
of which had removed a large portion half-way
up, it still withstood our attempts to destroy its
base, for I wanted to bring it all down together.
At the same time the 4·7's kept up a steady fire
upon 41e to keep him quiet.

During the afternoon a Hun machine flew over
us and dropped three white fire-balls.   Knowing
that this was a ranging signal to their guns, we
moved back, but nothing arrived over.   They
said that the Germans take ranges of the fire-balls
which are dropped vertically over a target and
use this range as a basis.

At dusk we ran out and shelled the Auchy
Headquarters, and then went home.

During the afternoon the Germans began shelling Cuinchy again, and word arrived that an attack was preparing in front of the 2nd Brigade, so we opened fire with the 6-inch on the Auchy corner of the triangle and the 4·7 on the northern embankment till 10.30, when all was quiet again.

The sausage went up again in the direction of Coisne, so out we ran again to Pont Fixe, but he was descending and being hauled away before our first shell had burst. Of course, we had been seen coming and two batteries opened fire on the station. We got clear, however, and then they tried to hit the line behind us, so that our return was most exciting, for it was only possible to hear the crash of the explosion above the roar and rattle of the train travelling at a terrific speed, and to look around and say, " Where did that one go ?" Luckily the rails were not hit, or we should have made a nice pile of wreckage.

At dusk we bombarded for half an hour with the 6-inch guns on Douvrin and the 4·7-inch on Haisnes, both villages being used as rest quarters and reserve billets by the enemy.

The attack during the forenoon had been made by 600 troops of the 116th Regiment, who had till lately been facing the French at Hullock. A hundred of them were killed by our bombardment, but the remainder, carrying axes and scaling-ladders, rushed on against the " Keep." The

THE FAMOUS PONT FIXE BREWERY.

To face page 132.

Sussex were there and drove them off, leaving 1915.
fifty dead Germans around the position. The
Northamptons lost a bit of their trench at the
first rush, but, recovering, counter-attacked, and
killed every Hun in it. A prisoner taken stated
that large numbers of Germans had been killed
and wounded during the recent shelling of La
Bassée; this looked like a feather for us.

The 2nd Division's guns were registering on the Jan. 30th.
triangle during the next forenoon, so we were
quiet. The sausage, however, went up at Illies,
so we at once ran out before he could get too high.
This time we were able to get five bursts near him
before he was run to the rear and pulled down.
The usual reception greeted us on arrival at Pont
Fixe, but we got through again without a hit after
another exciting dash home.

The afternoon arrived with no apparent dis-
turbances from the enemy, so we had another
trial against the chimney, getting two more hits
out of fifteen rounds; but it still stood up. Meanwhile No. 57c—a new position containing two
5·9 guns which had been firing on us lately—was
kept quiet by the 4·7's.

A quiet day followed, during which we watched
one of our 9·2 howitzers registering on the triangle.
One of its shell fell into a Hun trench and delivered
a Boche into the Munsters' trenches. The 169th
Regiment had by now been withdrawn from our

1915. front because of its heavy losses on the 25th, being relieved by the 112th Regiment. During the night a party of them rushed an advanced post held by the Coldstreamers, and still held it in the morning in spite of a counter-attack.

The howitzers put down a ten minutes' stream of high-explosives, and then a party of Irish and Coldstreamers rushed forward, retaking the post, and passing on gained the other one we had lost on January 25th, making prisoners of an officer and thirty-one men, and capturing two machine guns, all that remained of a company which had set out the night before; so that, one way and another, this had been an expensive amusement for the Hun.

All that forenoon I had been unable to fire, as the London Scottish were waiting alongside us as a reserve in case of need during the attack. All was clear in the afternoon, when orders came to engage 41e and 59, as they were shelling our forenoon's gains. This went on till things quietened, at 3 p.m., when we turned on to the chimney again, this time bringing it crashing down with a third hit and thirteenth round, the brick-dust from its fall putting a red cloud over the triangle.

On my return that evening I heard that it was intended to relieve the 1st Corps by the 2nd Corps, and also that my train would probably go back, so that our activities were to stop for a while; it had been very interesting in spite of the cold and 1915. awful rains. General Fanshawe paid us some nice compliments, and said he was sending a report to Littlejohns.

This report reads:

" 1ST DIVISION,
" *February 1st,* 1915.

" The armoured train has been in action daily and has done much good work against the triangle and the German guns about La Bassée and Auchy. The shooting has been good, and several direct hits have been scored. To-day a high chimney used by the Germans as an observation station was brought down. When a German captive balloon has gone up out of range of any of the guns of the Division Lieutenant R—— has taken his train up to Pont Fixe and obliged the balloon to come down.

" The train has received a great deal of attention from the German guns, but by judicious handling it has so far escaped injury.

" (Signed)   E. A. FANSHAWE,
" *Brigadier-General,* 1st *D.A.*"

A day's downpour intervened, and then I Feb. 4th. motored to Boulogne for a conference, returning in time to go out on the afternoon of the 4th and open fire on a factory and another chimney to the north-eastward of the triangle, scoring several hits, but no definite result.

The troops of the 2nd Corps, under General

1915. Haig, were gradually taking over the line from the 1st Corps, and many troops were in the area, so that little firing was done. However, I was able to continue against the same target with the 6-inch, keeping 57c quiet with the 4·7's until after the twenty-second round the chimney crashed down, on its way knocking down the whole western wall and roof of the factory, which had already been made very rickety by our misses. Now the interior was in full view, so that it was rendered useless for cover and shelter.

Feb. 6th.   An operation by the Guards Brigade was planned for the afternoon of the 6th, commencing with the registration of " Mother "—our 9·2-inch howitzer— upon the triangle's embankment and some brick-stacks held by the enemy. For a quarter of an hour prior to the attack the whole Corps artillery joined in, the result being a huge area of explosions, fire, and brick-dust, all forming an immense red cloud covering the entire front. Our own particular job was the holding up of reinforcements by a barrage on the canal bridge and the far apex. At 2.15 p.m. the Coldstreamers rushed the brick-stacks, and the Irish the trenches on their right. Within three minutes General Lord Cavan had won a further addition to his increasing bunch of successes, for the whole of the objective had been secured by his men, as well as twenty survivors of the original defenders, also a machine gun and

a trench mortar. Indeed, some units had gone 1915.
too far and had to be brought back. So helpless
had the enemy become that our Sappers were able
to go out and erect 300 odd yards of wire before
dusk, so that our line was now securely held east
of the brickfield.

Soon after the attack had been launched we
shifted our fire on to 41e to keep Fritz quiet, some
of our shells causing fires to break out around the
canal bridge at this corner of La Bassée.

Shortly before 3 p.m. we again shifted the 4·7's
on to Haisnes, which, being the position of the
reserve troops, might also be the point of assembly
prior to a counter-attack, so we put the 6-inch on
the triangle communication trench.

Through the whole period the hostile fire in our
area had been confined to a few " woolly bears "
scattered harmlessly all round, but before long
everything was quiet again and all shelling ceased.

An hour later we got orders to shell the interior
of the triangle, for prisoners had stated this area
was full of troops, so we opened fire with this object,
till forty minutes later all the artillery was put
on to Auchy, where quite two battalions had been
seen preparing to attack; our fire dispersed them
and the attack never materialized. Our total
casualties for the day's work was only twenty.

Upon return that evening to Bethune, I had a
farewell dinner with the Brigadier, and thereafter

1915. came under the orders of the C.R.A. of the 2nd
Corps, General Onslow.

The Commander-in-Chief sent a telegram to all
the artillery which had been working under the
1st Corps during the last six weeks, congratulating
them on their good work.

During that night a party of the enemy were
seen approaching the front of the Coldstream
Guards, who allowed them to come within a few
dozen yards of their wire and then opened fire;
thirty dead were found at daylight.

Quietness was the order of the day following our
success, and it looked as if we were in for a rest,
till about 4 p.m., when the enemy put down a
heavy fire upon the Cuinchy front. As this increased in intensity, I joined in the reply by
opening fire with the 6-inch on Auchy and the
4·7's on the southern apex. In our area large
shells were ploughing into the wood on the left
and along the canal, a couple of bursts unfortunately getting into some troops who were passing
at the time. Before an hour had passed all was
quiet again, and we learnt that a hostile attack
had been launched, but was dispersed by the
artillery's quick action. That evening I had an
excellent and amusing dinner with the Divisional
Cavalry—the XVth Hussars.

A successful attack by the French on our right,
to improve their position and get up more into

the lines with us, followed, and then several days 1915.
of wind and rain prevented all operations.

During this time the Belgian 4·7-inch section
arrived under Captain Servais to relieve us, and on
the 12th I took him and his observer to the O.P.
to show them the points of note and explain the
working of the O.P. and other details. At the
same time we continued our attempt to destroy
the bridge, but soon after starting this the enemy
shelled the O.P. so heavily that our observer had
to retreat to the cellars. We got going again later,
but beyond sending various girders flying and
doing similar less vital damage, even ten direct
hits did not eat away enough of the support to
cause it to collapse; a few 9·2 howitzer hits were
necessary. That night I introduced Servais to the
Staff he was to work with, and then I waited over
a day or two to assist him to settle down in his
new surroundings, strange after his experiences
when working with his own people on the Yser.

After another wild and wet day, Servais took his Feb. 14th.
section out, and I went on with his observer to
the O.P. to assist during the usual bombardment
prior to a successful but restricted attack by the
infantry near the brickfield. From this position
in the O.P. the advance and the fighting could be
seen and followed much as a spectator in the grand-
stand watches a football match. Through flashes
could be seen every detail and movement of the

1915. fighters, even to the expressions on the faces, all
seeming like the dumb-show of a cinema film: a
rifle pointed, and a spit of flame from the muzzle
without hearing the report, and officers obviously
giving orders and gesticulating. Not that we were
too far off to hear such sounds, but they were
drowned in the continuous roar of the battle itself.
The struggle was interesting and exciting, even
from a spectator's point of view, and more so
from my own, as I was playing a part in the great
game going on in front of me. Beyond our line
of trenches white puffs of smoke continually burst,
the shells passing overhead in a succession of
rushing shrieks. Larger black volcanoes of mud
and flame showed the fall of high-explosives
destroying the enemy's line, whilst occasionally a
flash and a huge red dust-cloud would show where
one had landed in a pile of bricks.

All along the front, on both sides, our own and
the German batteries were pouring down their
shells, each battery dependent for the accuracy of
its fire on its observer situated similarly to myself.
In a few moments a stir was apparent in the British
line, a glimpse of a row of khaki figures clambering
from their trench and the flicker of their bayonets,
and in an instant the ground beyond was dotted
with moving figures, making a fair target for the
German rifles and machine guns—such as had
survived the bombardment.

Figures sprawled, some never to move again, 1915. others to rise and stumble on after their comrades, as yet more fortunate in being untouched.

The advance having started, the fighting-line surged forward, checked and halted, moved again —now rushing, now staggering, and so on till the edge of the German trench became dotted with bobbing heads and moving figures, the next moment to be hidden by the swarm of our men as they leaped upon them.   Then suddenly this area became the object of the enemy's artillery, endeavouring to shell out the survivors of the victorious attackers and prevent the consolidation of the position won.   Now it was our turn to look round and engage the enemy's guns and try to check their design.

We saw target No. 11 in action and attempted to get the train on to this objective. A large error in direction at the start looked suspicious, and upon return to the train I found the new bearing racers were a matter of 2 degrees in error, a fault which I corrected before leaving.

Next day we returned to Boulogne, and were able once more to send some of the men, a few at a time, home on leave again. As for myself I got to London for four days on March 1st.

CHAPTER V

NEUVE CHAPELLE

1915. RETURNING from leave, I had to take charge of the work of completing the mounting and equipment of the new 4-inch guns which had arrived from home. This completed, the guns were sent out to join Gould; and I then carried out the erection of the 6-pounder from my train on a cliff west of the harbour of Boulogne, to reinforce a couple of French small pieces there for the defence of the port against U-boat attacks—our own men manning one gun day and night.

From now on I was directed to act as Gunnery Officer of all the sections, a job which included inspection of each unit at intervals, and of the preparations prior to the coming offensive on our own centre before Lille. For use in getting about the country I was provided with an Austin four-seater, a new car which gave me much pleasure in my efforts to obtain an up-to-date knowledge of driving under varying and often difficult circumstances.

Mar. 7th. On March 7th I set out for the train under Gould, and after reporting on the way at a

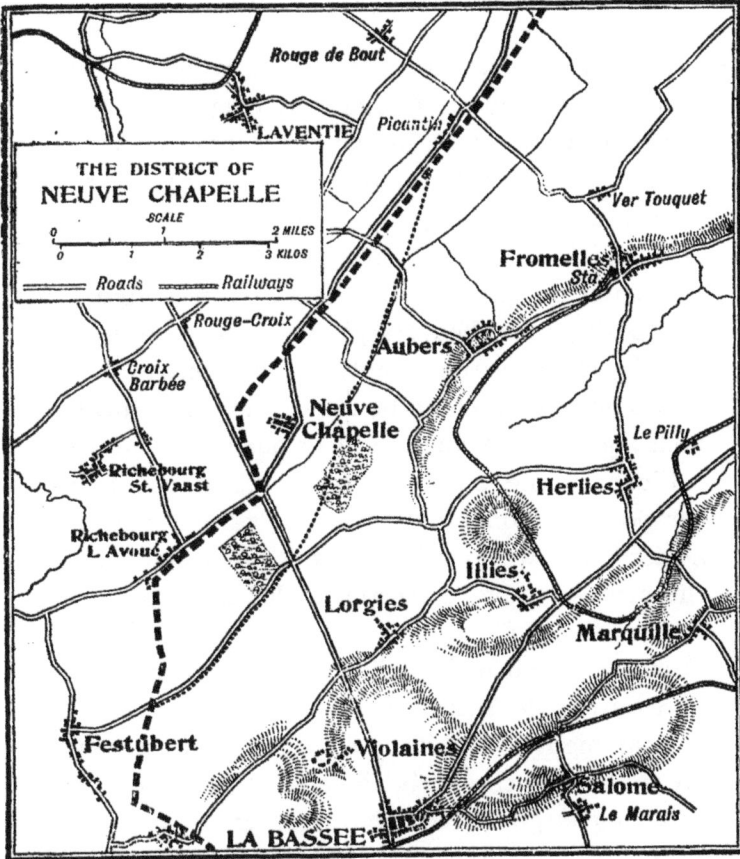

THE DISTRICT OF
NEUVE CHAPELLE

SCALE

0   1   2 MILES
0   1   2   3 KILOS

═══ Roads ═══ ════ Railways

Rouge de Bout

LAVENTIE   Picantin

Ver Touquet

Fromelles
Sta.

Rouge-Croix

Aubers

Croix
Barbée

Neuve
Chapelle

Le Pilly

Richebourg
St. Vaast

Herlies

Richebourg
L'Avoue

Illies

Lorgies

Marquilles

Festubert

Violaines

Salome
Le Marais

LA BASSEE

1915. couple of the Headquarters under which we were to work, reached La Gorge that evening. During the following day we sought out a position for the train when in action, and an O.P. in Laventie from which we could get a good view of the country over which the attack was to take place and our particular targets. Laventie Church was an excellent position for the latter, but too likely to become the object of hostile attention; however, we found that a good view could be obtained from a turreted house near by, so there fixed up our telephones, etc.

Close to the position of the train, which was composed of one 6-inch, one 4·7-inch, and two 4-inch guns, we found the new 15-inch howitzer in the process of being erected under the supervision of R. Bacon (Temporary Colonel, R.G.A.). His observer joined us in our O.P. and used this position during the next few days.

That night I reported to General Montgomery, my friend of the early days of Ypres, who was now in charge of the southern group of heavy guns; and on the morrow visited the train still working under Servais before La Bassée.

That night the orders for the attack were issued. Our positions lay just to the west of Neuve Chapelle, which village was the first objective, whilst the Aubers Ridge beyond was then to be attacked, from whence an advance on to the plain of Lille would threaten the city, and also outflank La

Bassée in the south. Three hundred guns of 1915.
calibres varying from " Grandmother," the 15-inch
howitzer, down to the small 12-pounders, were
arranged in a large circle so that their converging
fire could be directed upon the centre at Neuve
Chapelle. The attacking troops were the 4th
Corps under General Rawlinson and the Indian
Corps under General Willcocks, whilst simultaneously the 2nd Army at Ypres and the 1st at
Givenchy were to carry out a holding offensive
to prevent the enemy from drawing upon these
neighbouring sectors for reinforcements with which
to meet the main attack.

At 7.30 a.m. the first gun opened fire, and soon Mar. 10th.
all 300 guns were concentrated upon the trenches
and defences round Neuve Chapelle. The earth The First
vibrated as if struck by a huge hammer. The first
shells that hit the enemy's position raised a cloud
of smoke and dust, so that throughout the bombardment we could see nothing but a mass of
greenish lyddite fumes and great tongues of red
flame and flying earth. Defences and parapets
crumbled like sand, and revolting fragments of
human flesh were scattered in every direction.
For fully thirty-five minutes our gunners worked
at full speed, expending more ammunition than
in eighteen months of the Boer War, and at the
end of it there were no defences—only blasted
earth and mangled bodies.

1915.   Our own particular targets included the batteries
at Bas Pommereux, Aubers, the Aubers-Fromelles
road, and the exits from Aubers; also the Aubers
Church, which was a commanding hostile O.P.
overlooking our advance.   This latter was also a
target for the 15-inch, the first round from which
missed to the left, but completely demolished a
factory; before it could be loaded and fired again
we had hit the target six times with our 6-inch
and set the steeple alight.   The second round from
the giant howitzer detonated on the road beyond
the church, demolishing several houses.   The zone
of its destruction appeared to grow gradually just
like the ripples on the surface of a pond when a
pebble is dropped into it.

When the preliminary bombardment was over,
all guns lengthened their range on to the various
targets and the village itself.   The houses began
to leap into the air, and huge brick and dust clouds
rose up to the heavens; trees fell like grass, and
the consequent blanket of smoke and débris in
front grew denser and denser.   Then the whistles
blew all along the line and the infantry started
their advance.

All day long Gould and myself continued
observing from this position, though several stop-
pages were caused by breaks in our telephone lines
to the train when hit by shells.   Hostile guns were
shelling Laventie, and the church and cross-roads

behind us were getting a particularly warm time. 1915.
As the day progressed news gradually filtered
through, keeping us informed of our steady advance. Our troops had practically walked through
the demolished German defences, experiencing little
opposition from the few half-demented survivors
of the awful bombardment; and passing through
the remains of the village, established themselves
on the eastern outskirts, but the left was experiencing some difficulty from uncut wire. Similarly the
Indians had advanced after some checks, and now
were in line with their neighbours on their left.
Front of our O.P. the constant stream of fireworks
and Verey lights—sent up by our men to indicate
their positions, and by the enemy as signals to
their own guns to come to their assistance—made
a brilliant but confusing display.

Towards noon the firing had appeared to slacken,
and we could see several of our batteries moving
forward—an encouraging sign. Again in the afternoon our troops attacked and everywhere advanced, but towards dusk the battle seemed to
lessen in intensity of the rattle of rifle and battery
fire, and we heard that a check had occurred.

Details arrived in due course. The 7th and 8th A Check.
Divisions had been held up near the Moulin du
Pietre and by the small stream—the Des Layes.
The Indians had more than once cleared the Bois
du Biez, but each time had to come back to the

1915. alignment of those held up on their left. In the
neighbourhood of the Des Layes were more strong
positions which our guns had not yet touched, and
to push an infantry attack would have been need-
less sacrifice. So as the evening was closing in
we devoted ourselves to strengthening our line on
the ground won. Neuve Chapelle was ours; we
had straightened out our line and advanced a mile.
But we had not broken through, and valuable
hours were slipping by.

Mar. 11th. The plan as arranged for the morning was that
the 4th Corps was to attack the Les Mottes Farm
and pass on to Aubers, whilst the Indians were to
clear the Bois and wheel to the right upon Halpe-
garbe. But bad luck continued to follow us, for
Foiled by the morning arrived with a heavy mist over the
Weather. whole country. Artillery fire was lively on both
sides, especially from the enemy farther south.
Our own job was to keep up a fire upon Aubers
to check reinforcements, and to try and locate and
then engage hostile batteries. The first was simple,
but the second almost impossible, for the mist shut
out the view. The enemy made an attack from
the Bois early in the morning, but were easily
driven off by the Indians. Our own advance,
however, was impossible on any large scale without
the proper artillery support, which the mist prevented. All were very disgusted at this bad
luck, for every hour's delay gave the enemy

LAVENTIE CHURCH BEFORE THE BATTLE.

LAVENTIE CHURCH AFTER THE BATTLE.

To face page 148.

more time in which to bring up reinforcements 1915. against us.

The following day was a little better, though the Mar. 12th. fog lay over the country in the morning, but during the afternoon it gradually cleared, and the artillery became very active on both sides, our targets remaining as before.

Throughout the day several messages brought us the news of attacks and counter-attacks, each side fighting hard; the incessant roar of the guns, the rattle of rifles and machine guns, and the continued display of fireworks indicated this. But we were only able to move forward in places, getting up as far as the Moulin du Pietre. Laventie got its fair share of the shelling, though many were fortunately duds.

A small house alongside our O.P. was occupied by a couple of women and some children, who sat there all day quite fearless, notwithstanding that all the houses on the opposite side of their street and around the church were blown to bits. During the afternoon the Field-Marshal visited the train.

That evening Estaires was full of German prisoners and our wounded. The casualties on our side had been heavy indeed, but the Germans had lost even more; in fact, in front of our regiments a whole German battalion lay dead—a thousand corpses over a hundred yards' front. The questioning of prisoners was held in the Hôtel de Ville,

1915. and to relieve the congestion of the streets several
hundreds were taken to some barges on the canal,
but they could not be persuaded to go on board,
for they declared that once there we would sink
the barges and drown them all, for they had been
told by their officers that we killed our prisoners.

Two young German cadets had just been sent
to this front in charge of a draft of reinforcements;
they had been awakened in their billets by our
opening bombardment, and set out to move forward to join up with their unit in front. Approaching Aubers, they ran into our fire and hid
in the woods till dark, when they again moved
forward, got lost, and walked straight into our
lines, whence they were led to our rear, prisoners,
and never having fired a shot in their short
career.

We heard that during the preceding night the
6th Division just north of us had created a diversion and had captured L'Epinette.

Mar. 13th.   Saturday morning was almost as bad as the
preceding two days, for the mists were still low
and thick. We continued to keep a steady fire
on our targets and upon Fromelles. The shelling
around us became more violent, and our O.P.
looked like being demolished. It had already
been hit, so that one side of the house had collapsed
and the gardens around were full of holes by now.
However, the building continued to bear a charmed

life and lived through it.   All the news we could 1915.
obtain was that our offensive movements were
stopped for the present, and that the hostile
strength was increasing.   Next day the whole
operation was finally abandoned.   The delays
caused in the first case by the wretched bad luck
of the weather had given the enemy sufficient time
to bring up so many reinforcements that attacks
now would be at far too costly a price.

Later on Gould and myself went into Neuve
Chapelle itself to visit the scene of the battle.
We had some narrow squeaks from snipers who
were still hiding in the ruins, for being still dressed
in the blue naval uniform we made good targets.
Arriving at the remains of the German lines, we
found an awful sight of ruin and slaughter.   At
the time this area was being held by the Rifle
Brigade in reserve and a Scottish regiment was
clearing up the mess.   The German trenches, or
rather what was left of them, were full of dead,
four and five corpses deep, whilst the shell-holes
and dug-outs were littered with hundreds lying
and sitting in all manner of positions—almost every
face showing signs still of indescribable terror.
Hardly a square yard remained untouched by our
bombardment.   In our conspicuous rig we made
too good an aiming mark to go to the front line,
but in and around this ruined village we saw quite
enough to last us a lifetime.   At the same time

1915. the one thing most remarkable was the extra-ordinary high spirits of the soldiers.

The vigour of our offensive had put new heart into them after the wretched winter. The feeling that at last they were going forward more than repaid their losses, the wounded themselves think-ing not of their own afflictions, but spinning wild yarns of the day's incidents. During the first rush our men crowded into the hostile trenches, all eager to take some part in the fight, and none more so than the Indians, who now could fight in methods more in keeping with their spirit and custom.

Not less marked and noteworthy was the revealing of the conditions under which the enemy had existed during the previous winter. The trenches were narrower than ours and deeper, with quite a foot or more of water in them, but the dug-outs were most comfortable. This contrast might indi-cate the German officer's custom of looking after his own comfort first and leaving the men to shift for themselves. Furniture and every sort of utensil were to be seen everywhere, probably all having been removed from the village behind.

That evening I returned to Boulogne to prepare my own train for service, as one was required for some particular work on the Belgian Front.

CHAPTER VI

THE YSER, 1915

During the evening of March 18th I arrived with 1915. the train of three 4·7-inch guns, etc., at Dunkerque, and reported on the following day to the British Mission at the Belgian Headquarters, a member of which took me on to the Headquarters of the 3rd Division of the Belgian Army, General Jacques, under whom I was to be placed. The Division held the sector in front of Dixmude. It was arranged that I should use a siding at Bray Dunes as a resting place for the train during daylight, for the operations were all to take place at night. I had a Rolls-Royce attached to the train for use in reporting daily at the Headquarters. I was to have the services of three different Belgian observation posts, each of which was to report the lines of direction of our bursting shell; these reports were plotted at a central station and any error reported to me for correction. Such an ideal system of spotting promised to produce good results.

Early in the evening of the 21st we advanced Mar. 21st. to abreast the Cambron Farm on the Dixmude line and connected up the telephone, getting into

1915. touch with the Headquarters and O.P.'s. When
everyone was ready the guns moved on to K. 24,
laying the connecting telephone line as they advanced. We were so close to the front lines that
I kept the guns and the unarmoured sections well
separated; my office was in the latter section, in
which the reports of the spotting or any revision
in targets or orders from the Headquarters were
received, and working from my maps there I could
telephone the firing orders to the guns in front.

Shortly after 10 p.m. we ranged on to Beerst
Village, and then bombarded this area with forty
rounds, this firing being the only item of our night's
programme.

The following evening we were out in position
by midnight, but our rôle was merely to be ready
to open fire as ordered, in case our assistance was
required in a small operation which was timed to
take place at 2 a.m. At this time rifle-firing
suddenly broke into the stillness of the night, but
all was dead silence again by 2.45 a.m., very little
artillery fire having been seen. When dawn began
to break we returned home.

Mar. 23rd.   By ten o'clock the same night all were ready
with the guns at K. 24. The nights at this time
were most extraordinarily clear and brilliantly
illuminated by a full moon, and any tendency to
become drowsy during the long silent periods of
waiting was checked by the sharp frosts.

Shortly before eleven we opened fire, ranging on 1915. Beerst, and, using this index, carried out a ten minutes' bombardment of two battery positions— No. 42, a pair of 8·3-inch howitzers, and No. 27, one of small calibre. The atmosphere was ideal for observation purposes, our bursting shells being very spectacular. The common shell produced a huge brilliant hanging flame which was easily spotted, but the T.N.T. a quick yellow flash which was almost too quick to draw a bead on. Towards the close of our firing a few small shells from some field gun burst around our position, but well clear, and at midnight we went home.

Twenty-four hours later we went out again, Mar. 25th. waiting with the guns as far forward as K. 23·4, which was only 1,000 yards in rear of our trenches. At 1 a.m. we ranged upon Vladsloo and Beerst, and then burst into rapid firing upon the former village and No. 42 target. A shower of bullets from the enemy's infantry came over, but being spent, flattened out on the armour. The firing over, the train retired to K. 24·8, and we had to keep quiet till 3 a.m., when, ranging on Keyem, we followed up with a rapid burst on that village and target No. 27.

All these villages were entirely used as rest camps and reserve billets for the Germans, who must have been getting fed up now at having their nights so much disturbed by us. The firing

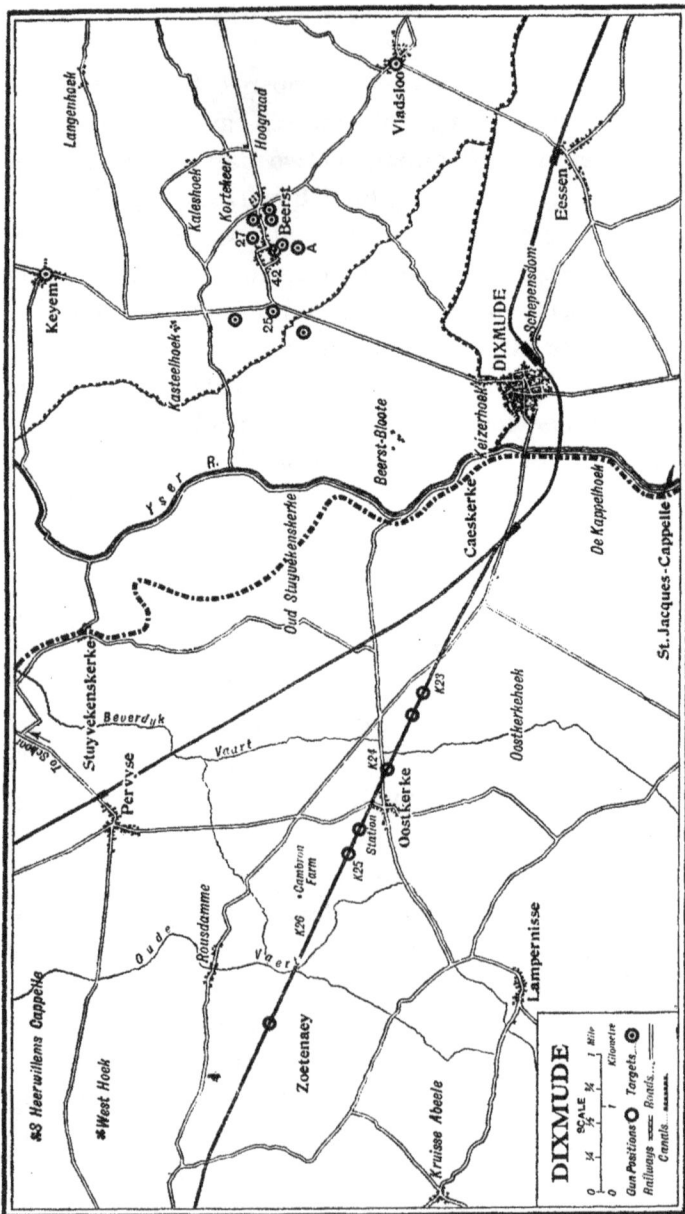

DIXMUDE

SCALE

0 ¼ ½ ¾ 1 Mile
0   1 Kilometre

Gun Positions ◉ Targets ⊙
Railways ⊐⊐⊐⊐ Roads........
Canals ⌐⌐⌐⌐⌐

on No. 42 had been particularly good; our first 1915 round was spotted 5 yards clear of one emplacement, so probably the unpleasantness of this shoot was the cause of the battery being moved during the following day to another position, as was later observed.

During the day I was introduced to H.R.H., who was much interested in our landship and her mode of working.

Midnight found us ready, the guns being as far forward as possible at K. 23, beyond which the lines were destroyed. At 1.10 a.m. we opened fire on K. 42*a*, getting a hit with the third round; after which we burst into rapid fire for three-quarters of an hour, taking in turn No. 27, Hoograad houses and cross-roads, and the route to Roulers. A great commotion was observed in that part of the field, fires breaking out here and there, and lights flitting to and fro showing the panic going on as they tried to get clear. A hostile battery opened fire on the train, but the majority of the shell burst or fell short, though one just missed one gun and fell behind it, and a very few only just short. During this night " Ermyntrude " wandered away on a prowl and only turned up towards dawn. " Jack Johnson " was out in the train with us that evening, and wrote the following yarn, which appeared in a periodical paper under the heading—

" Somewhere in France.

1915.   " It is many months since I first made the
acquaintance of Robert E. Lee.   Robert E. Lee,
I should explain, is a highly respectable, hard-
working armoured train of unimpeachable reputa-
tion, and so called because the Boches are fre-
quently waiting for him, but (for many reasons)
they will most certainly never catch him.   And
lest the Censor is growing apprehensive, I will
hasten to assure him that wild curates will not
drag from me the locality where Robert billets
and has his being, nor will any information likely
to prove of interest to the enemy escape my
discreet lips.

" There is something about an armoured train
that fires the imagination.   People like to think
that you can sit comfortably in the dining-car
eating veal cutlets while bullets and things bounce
off the roof and steel window-blinds like hailstones
off a tiled outhouse.   The idea thrills them to the
core.   Others, again, are intrigued by the delightful
fact that the Government have hired you a special
train for your own convenience to do exactly what
you like with and no officious guard to hustle you
aboard when you would tarry awhile and stretch
your legs at a wayside station.   Incidentally, it
may be noted that heavy pipe-smokers find an
armoured train a useful thing to strike matches on.
But this by the way.

" I well remember the first journey I was per-
mitted to make by the courtesy of Robert's commander.   My primary sensation on boarding the
train was one of reckless abandon.   The whole

train was at my disposal. I could sit in (what 1915. corresponded to) a first-class carriage with an old third-class return ticket belonging to the Great Eastern Railway, and there was nobody to make themselves disagreeable about it; I could even place heavy luggage (if I had any) upon the rack for light articles only. The novelty of the thing intoxicated me. I spent my first half-hour in throwing bottles on the line, travelling under the seat, leaning out of the window, leaving and entering the train when in motion, throwing orange-peel at the engine-driver, and pulling the communication cord (£5 or forty days).

" The outstanding characteristic of the armoured train is the ability to shake itself about in such a way that it is always in two places at once, and never in the spot where you would have bet a fiver that it would be, and where it might have been if it hadn't hustled out of it five seconds before. In this way, after loosing off your guns at the foe, you have nothing left to do but to stand and shake with laughter while you watch the enemy's shells bursting harmlessly around the spot where you might have been if you hadn't moved off first, and where the foe fondly imagines that you still are. Owing to the darkness he has, of course, only the flash of the guns to give him a clue to his enemy's position.

" I should mention in passing that the emotions experienced in the human bosom while the train is performing its celebrated shunting act resemble nothing on this globular planet, and should make a strong appeal to old Indian Colonels endowed with a liver of which a Strassburg goose might

1915. well be proud; though it is true there come back to mind faded memories of a metropolis of dazzling white in the Shepherd's Bush near where lived a sinister contrivance known as a ' Wiggle Woggle,' which—as the man at the gate earnestly assures bashful youth with a fair escort on their arm— was ' guaranteed to shake the hairpins out of a lady's coiffure within thirty-five seconds. Step up and try your luck.' For this kind of lightning manœuvre you need a first-class engine-driver, a man gifted with imagination, a sense of humour, and a quick eye. For this reason men who in private life embrace the vocation of a juggler or a legerdemain expert are invariably selected for the work in preference to men of more mediocre attainments.

" Up to the time of my visit the personnel of Robert E. Lee had barely sustained a single casualty, a remarkable circumstance directly attributable by the men to the presence of ' Ermyntrude,' the train's cat, a sandy-haired feline with a docked tail. ' Ermyntrude ' has brought nothing but luck since her advent some seven months back. Before she had been twenty-four hours at the base, out of pure consideration she had passed on to the sentry for the night—a notoriously drowsy individual—a certain active little stranger which made it quite impossible for the man to drop off to sleep, thus undoubtedly saving him from an ignominious death. ' Ermyntrude ' has passed an adventurous life. Of French parentage, she was abandoned upon the entry of the Germans into her native home, and was subsequently found by her present protectors upon the retirement of the

enemy from that quarter. Her sympathies are
entirely pro-Ally, and if you wish to rouse her
from her complacency you have only to exclaim
in your throat, ' Himmel ! Kreuz ! Gott strafe
England !' and she will claw you down the cheek
in a moment.

" It is the habit of Robert E. Lee to sleep
soundly throughout the day and creep out with
the falling shadows in the prosecution of his deadly
mission. In this way he does not offend the eye
of the Huns. On the occasion of my visit we
started out from the base at eleven o'clock. At
frequent intervals throughout the earlier part of
the night we would drag fretfully to a halt and
remain rooted to the spot sometimes for half an
hour at a stretch.

" And so the long night would drag slowly to a
close, and with the first faint flush of roseate dawn
illuminating the heavens the order would be given
to ' Up Steam ' and ' All aboard for Dixie.'

" And just as Robert was about to bound forward in the direction of home and friends some-
body discovered that ' Ermyntrude ' was missing.
To return without ' Ermyntrude ' was unthink-
able. In a moment big strong men with screwed-
up lips, headed by the cook, were deploying in every
direction, rendering the dawn hideous with what
they fondly imagined to be sounds of endearment.
The minutes passed, but no sign of the missing
feline. Things were getting serious. Every
moment it was growing lighter, and it was only
a question of minutes before the Germans would
discern the lithe, sinuous form of Robert E. Lee

1915. in the gathering light. But it was impossible to abandon ' Ermyntrude ' to her fate. At this critical juncture the cook, who had returned to his den to begin to get some food ready, suddenly shot his head out of the window and announced in loud and blasphemous terms that that —— cat was at that moment gorging herself on the men's breakfast. ' Ermyntrude ' was safe.

" Yours ever,
" JACK JOHNSON."

A Good Shoot.   One of the ultimate results of this successful shoot was that No. 42 had yet again moved to a third emplacement, and No. 27 had also been moved by the following afternoon, information of which points I received from the Headquarters. During the afternoon I went out to the ruins of Pervyse and forward into the Belgian trenches and a couple of machine-gun posts in that sector. The village was quite destroyed, but the trenches were very comfortable. Communication with the advanced posts was very hazardous, for one had to walk along faggot paths and duck-boards built over the flooded country; the waste of water, concealing in its depths the horrors of an avenging death, presents a silent testimony of that act of self-sacrifice which only just stayed the invading hoards.

Mar. 27th.   In the early hours of the morning we went forward, and by 1.30 were ready at K. 24, just beyond Oostkerke, but not till 3 p.m. did we

"ERMYNTRUDE," MY CAT.

To face page 162.

begin, when, after ranging upon Beerst, we bombarded both batteries for ten minutes; and turned
then on to No. 25, a new target at the cross-
roads west of Beerst. A 5·9-inch battery replied,
but all shell fell quite 200 yards short. Many
did not burst; all one heard was a squelching
thud in the mud, whilst others exploded like
squibs. The guns were retired to K. 24·8, and
waited till 4 a.m., when we gave Keyem a ten
minutes' disturbance.

When we were due to leave, " Ermyntrude " was
again missing from the fold, and search high and
low brought no favourable results, so as dawn was
breaking, we had to leave her behind and get
home out of it.

During the afternoon I went out to the Oostkerke O.P.'s, amongst other items looking for the
cat in the ruins around, but not a sign of her was
to be seen. We were particularly disappointed,
for not only had she been a shipmate for so long,
but an interesting event was shortly to take place,
and I had reckoned upon the Red Cross Funds
going yet farther to windward by the proceeds of
the sale of such famous animals as kittens born
on our train.

We now had thirty-six hours' rest, not going
out till 10.30 on the Sunday evening. From K. 27
we opened fire on a new target, Schoorbekke
Bridge, which we were to attempt to destroy,

1915. but at the second round the communications leading to the O.P.'s were cut by shell-fire.

Mar. 29th.   By midnight we were still out, so began a bombardment of the village of Schoor. However, later on the lines were restored, so we tried again on the bridge, and luckily got a hit in before the lines were again cut, but we continued the firing. This break in the telephone system was still unrepaired when we withdrew at dawn. The same evening we were out again by 9 o'clock and ranged on a big howitzer position, No. A, from K. 25, at Mar. 30th. about 11 p.m. Once again the lines were interrupted and it was midnight before we got them restored again; but this time we got on to the target and bombarded it. The 5·9-inch came over at us again, and though some fell both short and over, none were too near.

At 2 a.m the guns moved on to K. 23, beyond Oostkerke, and after ranging on Beerst, bombarded the positions of 42b and 27a and the roads between them. This time the same battery continued to fire at the position we had been in before, but did not hurt the metals.

When we went out in the evening the artillery on both sides was much livelier than usual, and shrapnel was flying around. Shortly before midnight we joined in with the Belgian artillery in a co-operative shelling of the large howitzer and then went home.

OOSTKERKE CHURCH.

To face page 164.

Two days followed without any action, and I 1915.
lunched with the Divisional Commander. During
luncheon the King of the Belgians visited the
Headquarters, a German aeroplane choosing this
moment to drop some bombs round the area. An
Allied aviator was seen to be in pursuit, so that we
were able to watch a fine air fight, which ended
in the Hun falling 8,000 feet in flames. Pégoud
was the victor.

We were out the same night, and shortly after April 2nd.
midnight opened fire upon the cross-roads on the
Yser, east of the Vicogne Château. Mists hanging
over the river greatly delayed the observers, but
between one and two o'clock we were able to get
going.

Whilst at Headquarters that afternoon I was
told that as things were so much quieter now, it
had been decided to keep the train back for a
spell. However, I took the opportunity of sending
in a report on the excellent conduct of my driver,
who had done so well on January 25th, and also
my Belgian guard—both of whom were rewarded
with the Order of Leopold.

I learnt that I was soon to return to England,
and therefore said good-bye to the Headquarters.
The General was most kind in his remarks and
thanks, as also Commandant Petrie, the Divisional
Artillery Officer under whom I had directly worked.

The train was temporarily laid up at Bray-

1915. Dunes, and it was here that I said good-bye to my men, and returned in the car to Boulogne. A fortnight later I returned to England on leave, and having received another appointment, my experiences with the armies were brought to a conclusion, having extended over seven of the most interesting months of the campaign.

APPENDIX I

WORK OF THE ARMOURED TRAIN—ENEMY EXASPERATED

(*Extract from " The Times."*)

FLANDERS, *November 22nd.*—I sent you the other day a brief account of the armoured trains which are operating in Flanders under Naval Command. I spoke of their excellent work in shelling the German batteries within their reach. Their fire has apparently been more effective even than our own gunners supposed. The enemy is exasperated. Five German prisoners who were captured at Furnes a day or two ago declare that the Kaiser has offered 20,000 marks (£1,000) for the head of the Commander of the armoured train.

LIST OF THE PERSONNEL OF H.M.A.T. " JELLICOE "

STAFF:

> Lavers, Chief Petty Officer, Gunner's Mate.
> Roper, Able Seaman, Messenger.
> Clark, Able Seaman, Telephonist.
> Martin, Able Seaman, Telephonist.

167

4·7-Inch Gun " Nelson ":

> Dick, Petty Officer, Gunlayer.
> Hood, Leading Seaman.
> Payne, Able Seaman.
> Pakes, Able Seaman.
> Church, Able Seaman.
> Tooke, Able Seaman.

4·7-Inch Gun " Drake ":

> Blondel, Petty Officer, Gunlayer.
> Lewis, Leading Seaman.
> Read, Able Seaman.
> Sawkins, Able Seaman.
> Peet, Able Seaman.
> Mockett, Able Seaman.

4·7-Inch Gun " Howe ":

> Collard, Petty Officer, Gunlayer.
> Clayton, Leading Seaman.
> Gallon, Able Seaman.
> Estaugh, Able Seaman.
> Blackenridge, Able Seaman.
> Fothergill, Able Seaman.

6-Inch Gun " Hood ":

> Etheridge, Petty Officer, Gunlayer.
> Pay, Leading Seaman.
> Cox, Able Seaman.
> Harris, Able Seaman.
> Brown, Able Seaman.
> Southy, Able Seaman.
> Prentice, Able Seaman.

KAISER'S £1,000 REWARD—HAVOC OF THE BRITISH ARMOURED TRAINS

(Extract from the " Express.")

NORTHERN FRANCE, *Sunday, Nov. 22nd.*—Almost incredible as it may seem, the Kaiser has offered a reward of £1,000 for the body, dead or alive, of the officer commanding or directing the armoured train which has done so much to hamper the operations of the Germans.

Large as the amount may appear, it is small in comparison with the damage—moral as well as material—done to the German troops by the armoured train, and the Kaiser would, doubtless, consider even 20,000 marks well spent if it could rid him of such an obstacle to his advance.

Apparently, however, the Kaiser has overlooked the possibility that, even if he could catch the Commander of the train, plenty of other British officers would be ready to take his place.

The very fact of so large a reward being offered shows to what an extent the good shooting from the train must have affected the German operations; and the apparent impossibility of ever doing any serious harm to so mobile an enemy must be exasperating to the German Generals.

So far, the trains themselves and their gunners have escaped almost uninjured, but the damage they have done is known to their cost by the Germans who have come within range of the train's guns.

KAISER'S £1,000 PRIZE—PRICE ON HEAD OF ARMOURED TRAIN

(Extract from the " Daily Mail.")

NORTH OF FRANCE, *Sunday.*—Five German prisoners captured a few days ago made a statement to the effect that the Kaiser had offered a reward of £1,000 to any German soldier who would kill the Commander of the British armoured train that has wrought so much havoc among the ranks of the enemy in Northern France and West Flanders.

I understand that His Imperial Majesty is particularly exasperated at the destruction caused among his crack regiments by this novel and highly original method of warfare. The Commander upon whose head such a high price has been fixed may well feel flattered by this genuine if grudging appreciation of his work on the part of the enemy.

AN AUSTRALIAN GUNNER WANTED BY THE KAISER

(Extract from the " Egypt Times.")

Australia has got some reason to be proud over several important incidents in connection with the war. The sinking of the *Emden* is of course the big feather in her hat. The capture of Germany's Pacific possessions is a matter of no little consequence, but the fact that Kaiser William has felt

himself called upon to put 1,000 sovereigns on
the head of a young Australian officer in charge
of an armoured train at Ypres is a good third on
our list of peculiar gratifications. Emperor William puts iron on his own heroes in the shape of
crosses—he puts gold on our hero in the shape of
sovereigns. Lieutenant R—— is wanted by the
Kaiser. The Lieutenant happens to be exceptionally gifted in the handling of guns, and is one of
the best, if not the best shot in the British Navy,
so he was taken from his ship, where the intern-
ment of the German men-of-war had left him small
opportunity of showing his ability, and put in
charge of an armoured train well within reach of
the enemy.

Then the trouble began. It is one of the most
persistent worries the enemy had to encounter.
Lieutenant R——'s guns were like the Germans'
sins—they were always finding them out. The
probability is that this one smart Australian is
responsible for more damage to the Prussians than
any other single man on the job. So irritating
has Lieutenant R——'s train been that the Kaiser
has felt himself called upon to make a big offer
for him, dead or alive. Of course, the Lieutenant
would be cheap at the price mentioned, but he is
proud to be made the object of this rare distinc-
tion. By the way, Kaiser William has started a
new line of warfare—*i.e.*, attack by purchase.
How much will it cost him to buy off the British,
French, Russians, Belgians, and Serbians at £1,000
per head ?

APPENDIX II

ARMOURED TRAIN VICTORY—OVER-WHELMING FORCE WIPED OUT

(*A Press Cutting.*)

NORTH-EASTERN FRANCE, *Saturday*.—News has reached here of the forging of a further link in the chain of successes with which the Allies are slowly but surely ringing the enemy. This week a very considerable force of Germans were completely routed by an armoured train. A skirmish was in progress between a British regiment and about half a Division of Germans, a skirmish which was rapidly developing into a struggle of some consequence. The enemy's line had been driven forward, and though neither side was aware of the other's presence, the issue of the fight at this point and at that time was of the first importance.

Greatly, absurdly outnumbered, outnumbered in the proportions which always bring out the finest qualities· of our troops, the battle went bravely on for an hour or so. Though the enemy were able, through their numerical superiority, to make three parts of a ring round the handful of British, the single regiment held on doggedly and with that grim determination with which the Germans are now so painfully familiar. By all the laws of warfare our soldiers should have

regarded the position as hopeless and have retired
before an overwhelming force. Technically considered, the situation probably demanded a retreat.
Luckily, technical considerations are generally left
out of the reckoning when it comes to the real
thing. They held on and did an immense amount
of damage to the serried ranks which were steadily
hemming them in.

Then came the end—the end of the enemy.
Sudden as a thunder-clap, deadly as lightning, an
armoured train shot up the railway-line which our
men were holding. In the pied garb of blue and
brown and yellow, the many-hued coat which
makes our land cruisers practically invisible, it was
in the middle of the fight before the enemy had an
inkling of his danger.

And then came vengeance. Right and left the
wicked machine guns spat out death and destruction, sowing an ever-widening field of swift annihila-
tion. Broadside after broadside was poured into
the enemy's inner flanks, wreaking havoc among
the closely packed lines. The train moved on to
the ceaseless rattle of the machine guns, mowing
down the Germans at every yard, moved on and
through. When it came to a standstill at last
the thing was done. Most of the ring which had
tried to engulf a single regiment was lying in
motionless heaps on either side, the rest were
flying for their lives. The chameleon-like armoured
train had in a score of minutes wiped out some
10,000 Germans and played a big part in wreaking
vengeance on land for what the German sub-
marines have done at sea.

APPENDIX III

IRON CAVALRY—ARMOURED TRAINMAN'S DIARY—BLUEJACKETS' BOUTS WITH BEWILDERED ENEMY

(Extract from the " Daily Chronicle.")

NORTHERN FRANCE, *November* 12th.—A diary showing the peregrinations of a party of bluejackets since the fall of Antwerp has just fallen into my hands.

" It is written a bit rough-like, sir," said the tar apologetically to me, " but it is the truthful log of an armoured train—a train that has scared the German. They call us the ' moving base,' and we don't half laugh at them shelling the spot where we was five minutes ago and where we ought to be always, as they think. We calls ourselves the ' ragtime navy boys.' We are touring artists, and we have put it across those Hewlans and Barbarians something shocking, I can tell you."

The diary gives the movements of one of the armoured trains, and gives a glimpse of the excellent work done by it.

CHATHAM TO ANTWERP.

October 1st.—Left R.N. Barracks, Chatham— 14 gunlayers, 42 trained men, 14 seamen gunners. Left South Dock for H.M.S. *Engadine ;* found her coaling; got aboard safe *en route* for Ostend. During the time, steaming with lights out, we had the misfortune to run mud; but two destroyers skulking about towed us off. But was delayed three hours. But at last arrived about 12 noon Friday.

October 2nd.—The *Engadine's* ship's company gave us a good send-off, and we gave cheer for cheer. We found a train waiting for us, which conveyed us to Antwerp. We passed through Ghent, Bruges (Brugge), St. Nicholas, and Berekem, and arrived Antwerp 7.30 p.m. Belgian officers met us, and we crossed the river in a tug. We passed through the city to our quarters, which was a girl's high school that was converted into barracks. Received orders to be ready by 3 a.m., and went to the station to armoured train, which had on 4·7 guns and one aerial gun. We were told off for guns' crews. We made ourselves acquainted with our surroundings, and was then ready for any emergency. So, being tired, we turned in sail-loft attached to station.

October 3rd (Saturday).—Had breakfast and had a run up and see the position, and finished for the day.

October 4th (Sunday).—Left Antwerp in armoured train at 4 a.m. for Waerlos, where we was shelling all day. We brought down a war balloon at 8,600 yards. . . . We then returned to Antwerp, after being in action nine hours.

October 5th (Monday).—Shelling at Verdron all day. French joined us with centimetre guns. Belgian Captain asked for volunteers to rescue three refugees. It was carried out by some of us safe, but little girl shot through thigh.

AT THE BATTLE OF MELLE.

October 6th (Tuesday).—Lay at Antwerp all day resting. Left at 10 p.m. for Vieux-Dieu. The Belgians changing positions, we had orders to leave the guns, and walked to Hoboken, about fifteen miles. We crossed the river and threw our leather gear into it. We slept in brewery for one hour. The Colonel gave us a glass of Hollands, and then recrossed ferry for Hoboken Station. We then went right through to St. Nicholas. During the night the 4·7 guns rejoined us. We had expected the Germans had captured them, but they were not touched.

October 7th (Wednesday).—All armoured trains, French included, left for different routes: French guns and our 6-inch guns together, and then arrived Ostend 4.15 p.m.

October 8th.—Had breakfast Hotel Excelsior, and had to wait Ostend waiting orders.

October 9th (Friday).—Still waiting orders. . . . Highlanders fired volley at German aeroplane, and brought it down.

October 10th (Saturday).—Started to dismount guns for shipment, but —— gave orders to reassemble gear. Left Ostend for Thourout, arriving 6 a.m. Sunday.

October 11th (Sunday).—Officer christened our guns Drake, Nelson, Jellicoe. Left Thourout for Ghent, arriving 4.30 Left for battle of Melle, the . . . in the trenches. We fired 30 rounds of shrapnel and 15 rounds of lyddite, covering the . . . retreat. We retired to Hansbeke for the night. Lieutenant was highly pleased with the night's work.

October 12th (Monday).—Cleaning out guns and getting for shelling. One 4·7 advanced under our fire and fired two rounds of lyddite. Stayed at Hansbeke till 7.30 p.m. and then returned to Athe. Belgians blew up Ghent Bridge.

" And Killed 'em All."

October 13th.—Waiting orders. Lieutenant went rounds; eight hands told off to transport English stores left at Ghent by . . . on to our armoured train. Left for Brugge. Civic Guard finished. Belgian Army *en route* for France. Left Brugge 3.15 for Roulers, arrived at 5 p.m. . . . Left Roulers for Dixmude, arrived 4 a.m.

October 14th (Wednesday).—Met other part of armoured train, which brought us ammunition from Dunkirk. Our 6-inch guns are at Dunkirk, under Lieutenant ——. Left Dixmude at 5.30 a.m. arrived Lichtervelde 8 a.m. . . . Left Lichtervelde, arrived Zonnebeke 12 noon. . . . 3 p.m. . . . fired on German aeroplane, brought it down, killing two officers.

October 15th.—Waiting orders at Ypres. Stayed all day a mile south of Frezemburgh, covering our artillery till they covered up their guns and got in position. Expecting to have a battle in the morning.

October 16th (Thursday).—Went to Houthem, at 12 noon. Dead horses on line and road, and lot of dead Germans. Captured one Uhlan and two infantrymen. . . . Went into action; shelled Germans one mile north of Comines.

October 17th.—At Houthem again. Villagers

12

digging holes in gardens burying household things.

October 18*th*.—Shelled Germans out of farm-house. They tried to blow up lines, but couldn't.

October 19*th* (*Monday*).—At Houthem again. Bombarded church held by Germans and killed 'em all.

October 20*th*.—Bombarding Germans at Zonnebeke. They had it hot and holy. . . . Called battle of Lille.

October 21*st*.—Germans retreated five miles from Zonnebeke. We shelled them all the way. It was murdering them, said an officer. Left for Poperinghe. Our Brigade hard pressed. Fired 30 rounds of lyddite and cleared Germans off. Our Division now advancing back.

October 22*nd* (*Thursday*).—Left Ypres for battle of Lille. Shelling all day. . . . Cavalry. Left for Zillebeke at 5 p.m.; fired 27 shrapnel and 21 lyddite T.N.T. at Germans for a nightcap.

October 23*rd* (*Friday*).—Shelled Germans out of Houthem. Fired 4 shrapnel and 28 lyddite T.N.T. Army officer brought fresh orders. A German battery is advanced, so we are off to put it out of action. Did it first round.

October 24*th*.—General clean-up in train.

October 25*th*.—Germans retreating from Houthem and Zonnebeke, and Belgian refugees going back home.

October 26*th*.—Five miles south of Zonnebeke blew up German big gun. Lieutenant said it was " Jack Johnson." Captured 50 prisoners and seven big guns. Prisoners sent to Havre; ages 16 to 19.

October 27th.—At Bethune for La Bassée.   Fired some rounds and drove off German attack.

October 28th (*Wednesday*).—La Bassée; put another German gun out.   French battery on our left put another out.   At night went to Ypres; in action 7 p.m. for seven hours.   Put 18 guns, three batteries, out of action.

October 29th.—Bombarding German batteries all day at La Bassée.

October 30th (*Friday*).—Shelled German infantry position.   Put 'em on the run at La Bassée.

October 31st (*Saturday*).—At La Bassée; put more German guns out of action.   Hundreds of 'em dead all around us !   God ! it was a sight !

After this the tar had a well-earned rest : but he was overjoyed when I last saw him, because he had just received orders to go to the front again.

" We are goin' in the mornin', sir," he exclaimed, " and by this time to-morrow night we will be chewin' 'ell into 'em !"

INDEX

BILLING AND SONS, LTD., PRINTERS, GUILDFORD, ENGLAND